英語総合教材

JAPAN EVOLUTION
進化する日本

ジョアン・ペロケティ

千葉　剛　　鄭　耀星

清水　雅夫　　林　孝憲

福岡　賢昌

共著

南雲堂
☎ 03-3268-2311

JAPAN EVOLUTION
© Copyright 2019
by
Nan'un-do Co., Ltd.

───── リーディング ‖ リスニングの力がつく ─────
JAPAN EVOLUTION
『進化する日本』
CD（全2枚）

─────［収録個所］─────

英文テキスト・練習問題 1, 2, 3

お近くの書店に注文のうえ、お買い求めください。

南雲堂

☎ 03-3268-2311

はしがき

　変遷する世界情勢と共に日本社会も進化し続けている。果敢に伝統的歌舞伎に革新を呼び起こしている松本幸四郎。日本の知性を代表する池上彰。日本の政治史上稀代の傑物、田中角栄。オバマ大統領の感動的なヒロシマスピーチ。多様化する IoT。金融効率化を促進しているフィンテック。ガンの救世主、オプジーボ。水中の生態系を解析する環境 DNA。美しい北限のつばき。岩手県が開発に成功した至上の米 "金色の風。" 働き方改革のストレスチェック。価格がリーズナブルなジェネリック医薬品。夢の自動運転車。無限の再生エネルギー。活躍する 3D プリンター等、いずれも貴重なテーマばかりであり、英語学習者の興味を本書が十分満たすものと思われる。

　英語の技能は、書く、話す、読む、聞くの 4 つに分けられる。本書は、主として読解力向上に主眼を置いているが、基礎的な英文法が学べるよう Grammar Review を入れた。また、英文の中に重要な語彙、イディオム、構文などをバランスよくちりばめて、多様性に富んだ英文が学べるように配置されている。練習問題は TOEIC® テスト形式にしているものもあるが、作成意図については 5 ページの「練習問題、文法解説の構成」を参照されたい。

　注釈に関しては、大学教養課程以上の単語や分かりにくい慣用句、専門用語を中心に解説を加えてある。従って、注釈にない語句や表現は、前後の文脈から類推して読み進めることをお薦めしたい。

　本書を著すに際して、南雲堂の岡崎まち子氏、加藤敦氏には、大変お世話になりました。ここに、編集者一同、心より御礼申し上げます。またイラストを担当して戴いた三輪美奈子氏にも感謝致します。

編著者

[参考文献]

Advanced American Dictionary, Longman, 2000

Macmillan English Dictionary, Macmillan, 2002

Random House Webster's Dictionary of American English, Random House, 1997

『エクシード英和・和英辞典』（三省堂，2004 年）

『現代用語の基礎知識』（自由国民社，2017 年）

『新英和大辞典』（研究社，2013 年）

『新選国語辞典』（小学館，2002 年）

『新編英和活用大辞典』（研究社，2005 年）

『スーパー・アンカー英和辞典』（学習研究社，2017 年）

『スーパー・アンカー和英辞典』（学習研究社，2017 年）

『ランダムハウス英和大辞典』（小学館，1994 年）

『リーダーズ英和辞典』（研究社，2007 年）

『ロイヤル英文法』（旺文社，2000 年）

『朝日新聞』

『産経新聞』

『日本経済新聞』

『毎日新聞』

『読売新聞』

International New York Times

The Japan News

The Japan Times

ER Synonym Dictionary Online 〈http://synonym.englishresearch.jp/index.html 〉

Longman English Dictionary Online 〈http://www.ldoceonline.com/ 〉

Merriam-Webster.com 〈https://www.merriam-webster.com/ 〉

Weblio 〈http://ejje.weblio.jp/ 〉

練習問題、文法解説の構成

練習問題 1（Comprehension Questions）

正確な英文理解が練習問題を解く鍵になるという視点から、TOEIC® テスト形式の内容理解の問題を用意している。

文法解説（Grammar Review）

読解と共に英文法の基礎を学習するという視点から、文法の重要事項を基本的な例文や本文からの引用文を用いて解説している。

練習問題 2, 3

読解における語彙の意味を類推することの重要性を考えて、適語選択問題、英文完成問題、穴うめ問題、同義語および反意語問題、単語の定義問題、そして語形変化問題等を用意し、語彙力が高まるよう工夫した。尚、答えが文頭に来るものも小文字で表示してある。また実践的な英語力を学習できるようリスニング問題も用意している。

《日本語の表記》

本文中の日本語は普通の活字体（ローマ字体）のままで表記してあるが、注釈にその説明をしてあるので参照されたい。

Contents

はしがき   *3*

1. Koshiro Matsumoto   *9*
歌舞伎を革新する松本幸四郎   文型

2. Akira Ikegami   *15*
日本の知性　池上彰   時制

3. Kakuei Tanaka   *21*
傑物　田中角栄   助動詞

4. Barack Obama's Hiroshima Speech   *27*
オバマヒロシマスピーチ   名詞・代名詞

5. The Internet of Things (IoT)   *33*
多様化する IoT   形容詞

6. Fintech   *39*
金融効率化　フィンテック   副詞

7. Opdivo®   *45*
ガンの救世主　オプジーボ®   比較

8. Environmental DNA　　51
生態系を解析　環境 DNA　　受動態

9. Camellia　　57
北限のつばき　　分詞

10. Rice　　63
至上の米　金色の風　　動名詞

11. Stress Check　　69
働き方改革のストレスチェック　　不定詞

12. Generic Drugs　　75
リーズナブルなジェネリック医薬品　　前置詞

13. Self-driving Cars　　81
夢の自動運転車　　接続詞

14. Renewable Energy　　87
無限の再生可能エネルギー　　仮定法

15. 3D Printers　　93
活躍する 3D プリンター　　関係詞

CHAPTER 1
Koshiro Matsumoto

松本幸四郎

　　Koshiro Matsumoto is a rising kabuki star. Born in Tokyo in 1973, Koshiro, like many kabuki actors, inherited his vocation and his name from his father. The "Koraiya" dynasty, founded by Koshiro I, dates back to the 18th century; the current Koshiro is the tenth actor to be honored with the name. In 1979, when he was just five years old, Koshiro made his acting debut at the Kabukiza Theater, Japan's best-known kabuki theater. Koshiro is also a talented stage and screen actor, with his remarkable acting versatility evident in portrayals of characters ranging from Hamlet, at age 14 in 1987, to Amadeus Mozart, in 1993, when he played opposite his father in the role of Salieri.

　　Koshiro has worked tirelessly to promote kabuki as part of Japan's overseas "Cool Japan" strategy. Over one weekend in August 2015, in Las

Vegas, Nevada, Koshiro gave five performances of the renowned kabuki classic, "Koi Tsukami" ("Fight with a Carp"). The production, which was staged outdoors, both preserved and broke with kabuki conventions. It attracted an international audience of more than 100,000 people who were enthralled by Koshiro's magnetic performances. Of the wildly successful production, Koshiro said: "I'd like to show people the potential power of kabuki."

What made the show particularly remarkable was its blending of modern technology with ancient tradition. The venue was a large artificial lake beside a popular hotel on Las Vegas Boulevard. The lake features the U.S.'s largest fountains, with over one-thousand air-pressure cannons and 200 underwater robots programmed to make the waters "dance." For Koshiro's production, the fountains' movements were choreographed to reflect the action taking place on the specially constructed stage. The show's original music was composed and recorded by musicians in Japan. Elaborate costumes and innovative computer graphics (CG) of carp projected onto giant "screens" of water heightened the dramatic experience.

A joint venture between Japanese and American corporations and artists, the three-day extravaganza aimed to expand awareness of the art of kabuki to worldwide audiences. The show was a free preview for an entirely new kabuki production, "Shi-Shi-O" ("The Adventures of the Mythical Lion"), scheduled to open next year.

Koshiro encourages young people to find one special thing that no one else can do and then to bring their dream to fruition through dedicated efforts.

Notes

9 ***Koshiro Matsumoto*** 「松本幸四郎」歌舞伎俳優。1973 (昭和 48) 年東京都生まれ。本名は藤間照薫。1979 (昭和 54) 年三代目松本金太郎を襲名して初舞台。1981 (昭和 56) 年七代目市川染五郎を襲名。2018 (平成 30) 年十代目松本幸四郎襲名。1987 (昭和 62) 年、史上最年少の 14 歳で舞台『ハムレット』に主演。2003 (平成 15) 年、芸術選奨新人賞。2005 (平成 17) 年、映画『阿修羅城の瞳』、『蝉しぐれ』に主演し、報知映画賞主演男優賞、日刊スポーツ映画大賞主演男優賞。2015 (平成 27) 年、浅草芸能大賞奨励賞。

1 **a rising kabuki star** 「期待の歌舞伎スター」

2 **vocation** 「天職」
 name 「名跡」芸名。

3 The "Koraiya" dynasty「高麗屋」
Koshiro I「初代幸四郎」1674（延宝 2）年〜 1730（享保 15）年。
dates back to「〜に遡る」
5 made his acting debut「初舞台を踏んだ」
6 the Kabukiza Theater「歌舞伎座」1889（明治 22）年開場。現在の所在地は東京都中央区銀座。
8 versatility「多芸ぶり」
Hamlet「ハムレット」シェークスピア作の戯曲『ハムレット』の主人公。
9 Amadeus Mozart「アマデウス・モーツァルト」ピーター・シェーファー作の戯曲『アマデウス』
の登場人物。作曲家モーツァルトのこと。
opposite「〜の相手役として」
10 his father「彼の父」二代目松本白鸚。1942（昭和 17）年東京都生まれ。本名は藤間照暁。
Salieri「サリエリ」『アマデウス』の登場人物。
11 to promote「広めるために」
as part「一環として」
12 "Cool Japan" strategy「「クールジャパン」戦略」日本文化を海外に広げながら、ビジネスに繋げ
ようとする国家戦略。
Las Vegas, Nevada,「ネバダ州ラスベガス」カジノ等のリゾート地として有名。
10 13 gave five performances「公演を 5 回行った」
14 "Koi Tsukami" ("Fight with a Carp")「『鯉つかみ』」歌舞伎狂言。主人公が鯉の化物を退治する
作品。
15 both preserved and broke with kabuki conventions「歌舞伎の伝統的慣習を守りそして破るとい
う両方（のスタイル）だった」
18 the potential power「底力」
20 the show「公演」
blending「融合」
21 venue「会場」
artificial lake「人口の湖」
22 a popular hotel「人気ホテル」カジノホテルのベラージオ。
Las Vegas Boulevard「ラスベガス大通り」カジノ、ホテルが並ぶ大通り。
features「売り物にしている」
23 fountains「噴水」
with over one-thousand air-pressure cannons and 200 underwater robots programmed to
make the waters "dance"「千以上の気圧噴水口と、噴水に「ダンス」をさせるようにプログラムさ
れた 200 の水中ロボットがある」
25 were choreographed to reflect the action taking place on the specially constructed stage「特設
舞台の上で行われる演技を反映するよう設定された」
28 Elaborate costumes「凝った衣装」
computer graphics (CG)「コンピューターグラッフィックス（CG）」プロジェクションマッピング。
29 projected onto giant "screens" of water「巨大な水の「スクリーン」に映し出された」
heightened「盛り上げた」
31 A joint venture「共同制作」
32 extravaganza「華麗な舞台」
awareness「認知度」
33 free preview「無料予告上演」
34 "Shi-Shi-O" ("The Adventures of the Mythical Lion")「『獅子王』」新作歌舞伎。宝剣を奪った怪
物と取り返そうとする兄弟獅子の戦いを描く。
36 encourages young people to find one special thing that no one else can do and then to bring
their dream to fruition through dedicated efforts「若者たちが他の誰にもできない一つの特別な
ことを見つけ、それからひたむきな努力を通じて自分の夢を実現させるように励ましている」

Exercise 1-1: COMPREHENSION QUESTIONS

1. What is the best description of Koshiro Matsumoto?
   (A) He is a veteran actor who has devoted his life to the stage.
   (B) He is a multi-talented and hard-working new star.
   (C) He is noted primarily for his overseas productions.
   (D) He accepts only roles in classical kabuki dramas.

2. What was especially important about the kabuki production in Las Vegas?
   (A) It gave the local economy a boost.
   (B) It was the first time a traditional kabuki play had ever been shortened.
   (C) It boosted Las Vegas's reputation as an entertainment capital.
   (D) It introduced kabuki to a large international audience.

3. Which of the following was NOT an element of the Las Vegas production?
   (A) Original Japanese music
   (B) Images of carp projected onto walls of water
   (C) The special performances in a large indoor arena for kabuki
   (D) Fountains choreographed to mirror the action in the play

4. How did the Las Vegas production differ from traditional kabuki productions?
   (A) It incorporated modern technology.
   (B) It was performed all in English.
   (C) The costumes were much less elaborate.
   (D) It included American performers.

5. Which of the following is TRUE?
   (A) New kabuki plays are no longer being written and produced.
   (B) Koshiro was discouraged because kabuki does not appeal to international audiences.
   (C) Modern performances of kabuki are likely to grow in popularity, thanks to artists like Koshiro.
   (D) Koshiro believes that young people should dedicate themselves to many different goals.

Grammar Review

Sentence Pattern
(文型)

be 動詞と一般動詞

be 動詞

1. 肯定文　現在形〈主語 + am/is/are + ….〉　過去形〈主語 + was/were + ….〉

    My father **was** a great sportsman. I **am** an outdoor person, too.

2. 疑問文　現在形〈Am/Is/Are + 主語 + …?〉　過去形〈Was/Were + 主語 + …?〉

    Was it really a UFO? **Are** you sure?

3. 否定文　現在形〈主語 + am/is/are + not + ….〉　過去形〈主語 + was/were + not + ….〉

    My mother **was not** fond of cooking. I **am not** a good cook, either.

一般動詞

1. 肯定文　現在形〈主語 + 現在形 + ….〉過去形〈主語 + 過去形 + ….〉

    主語が 3 人称単数(he/she/it)の時、現在形は〜 s/es。

    Ken usually **wears** jeans and a T-shirt, but he **wore** a suit and tie yesterday.

2. 疑問文　現在形〈Do/Does + 主語 + 原形 + …?〉過去形〈Did + 主語 + 原形 + …?〉

    Did you **sleep** well? **Do** you **feel** all right?

3. 否定文　現在形〈主語 + do/does + not + 原形 + ….〉過去形〈主語 + did + not + 原形….〉

    I **do not forget** things very often, but I **did not feed** my dog this morning.

5 文型

1. 第 1 文型(S + V)　動詞は目的語も補語も取らない完全自動詞。

    Koshiro has worked tirelessly to promote kabuki.
    　　　S　　V

    There is an American girl in our class. She comes from Hawaii.
    　　　V　　　　　　　　S　　　　　　　　S　　V

2. 第 2 文型(S + V + C)　S = C の関係。C は主格補語。動詞は補語を取る不完全自動詞。

    Koshiro Matsumoto is a rising kabuki star. He is also a talented screen actor.
    　　　　S　　　　　V　　　　　　　　C　　S　V　　　　　　　　　　　　C

    I felt sick, but I got better in a few minutes.
    S V C　　　 S V　 C

3. 第 3 文型(S + V + O)　動詞は目的語を取る他動詞。

    Koshiro inherited his vocation and his name from his father.
    　　S　　　V　　　　　　　O

4. 第 4 文型(S + V + IO + DO)　IO は間接目的語「〜に」。DO は直接目的語「〜を」。

    He asked me so many questions. (= He asked so many questions of me. [第 3 文型])
    S　 V　 IO　　　　　DO

    Koshiro encourages young people to find one special thing that no one else can do.
    　　S　　　V　　　　　　IO　　　　DO

5. 第 5 文型　O = C の関係。C は目的格補語。動詞は目的語を取る他動詞。

    She keeps her room tidy. Tidiness makes her happy.
    S　 V　　O　　C　　 S　　　V　　 O　 C

13

Exercise 1-2: Grammar Exercise

次の各文の文型を答えなさい。

1. Koshiro Matsumoto is a talented stage and screen actor.　　　第＿＿＿＿文型
2. Koshiro inherited his vocation from his father.　　　第＿＿＿＿文型
3. In August 2015, in Las Vegas, Koshiro starred in five performances of a special kabuki production over a long weekend.　　　第＿＿＿＿文型
4. A lot of kabuki fans call him "Koraiya."　　　第＿＿＿＿文型
5. The article told us what kind of man Koshiro was.　　　第＿＿＿＿文型

Exercise 1-3: Vocabulary Build-up

次の各語の定義として最もふさわしいものを（A）～（H）の中から選びなさい。

1. inherit　　　　　（　　）
2. versatility　　　　（　　）
3. preserve　　　　　（　　）
4. expand　　　　　（　　）
5. feature　　　　　（　　）
6. elaborate　　　　（　　）
7. strategy　　　　　（　　）
8. dedicated　　　　（　　）

(A) ornate; complex; highly decorated
(B) having many different skills; able to do many different things
(C) to have a quality or characteristic passed on to you from your parents
(D) a series of planned actions to achieve a goal
(E) determined; devoted to an aim or goal
(F) to keep something the same; keep from changing; maintain
(G) to include or show (or to be included or shown) as an important or recognizable part of something
(H) to make larger or more widespread

CHAPTER 2
Akira Ikegami

池上 彰

Akira Ikegami is one of today's most influential journalists. Some have called him "Japan's Intelligence." In one corporate survey, he was even named Japan's "Ideal Boss"! Born in Nagano Prefecture in 1950, Ikegami began his career as a reporter at NHK in 1973. From 1994 to 2005, the year he left public broadcasting to work as a freelance journalist, he hosted a special news program for children. Afterwards, he started to lecture at several universities. Throughout his long career, he has made clear communication his life's work.

Ikegami is a prolific author whose many books stress the importance of good communication. These include several best-sellers that explain the often thorny principles of economics in "digestible," reader-friendly terms. Using language that clarifies rather than obscures is no easy task, but Ikegami is a master of it. He credits his ability to communicate clearly to his years as a children's reporter. "Being able to 'translate' from Japanese to Japanese is the key to making news accessible," he has said.

It is also important to have a real understanding of the concepts behind technical terms. Another clear-communication tactic is to use experiences and ideas that audiences are familiar with as analogies for new and complex information. Likewise, using specific examples helps to make complicated situations and their underlying ideas more readily comprehensible. An economic issue like inflation, for example, becomes more understandable when it is presented so that audiences can see how it affects the family budget.

Ikegami is esteemed for his contributions to humanitarian causes. One in particular has been his work on behalf of the victims of the 2011 Great East Japan Earthquake. After the disaster, he often appeared on TV to clarify and console, and he donated the pay to victim relief.

In 1977, Megumi Yokota suddenly disappeared from her home, a victim of abduction by North Korea. In 2017, Akira Ikegami met Megumi's mother, offered her hope and encouragement, and spoke out on behalf of her and others in a similar situation: "The government must cooperate with the U.S. and the United Nations to solve these tragic cases."

Ikegami urges young people to become active citizens and, especially, to exercise their right to vote. "The 21st century is your age," he recently said. "If you go to the polls, our leaders will hear your voices, and develop policies that meet your needs."

Notes

15   *Akira Ikegami*「池上彰」ジャーナリスト。1950〈昭和 25〉年長野県生まれ。慶応義塾大学卒。NHK で社会部記者を務めた（1973 ～ 2005）。現在、東京工業大学特命教授。信州大学及び愛知学院大学特任教授。時事問題の著書多数。

2 **"Japan's Intelligence."**「「日本の知性」」

  one corporate survey「ある会社の調査」明治安田生命保険相互会社（1881〈明治 14〉年設立）が新社会人を対象に行うアンケート。

  was even named「～にさえ指名された」

3 **"Ideal Boss"**「「理想の上司」」

4 **a reporter**「記者」

5 **public broadcasting**「公共放送」

  freelance journalist「フリーのジャーナリスト」

hosted「司会を務めた」

6 **a special news program for children**「子供のための特別なニュース番組」『週刊こどもニュース』（1994 〜 2010）のこと。

9 **prolific author**「多作な作家」

11 **thorny principles of economics**「厄介な経済原理」

   "digestible,"「「こなれた」」分かり易い。

   reader-friendly terms「読者に分かり易い用語」

12 **obscures**「分かりにくくする」

16 13 **a master**「名人」

   credits「お陰だとしている」

15 **the key**「秘訣」

16 **concepts**「考え」

17 **technical terms**「専門用語」

   tactic「手法」

18 **audiences**「視聴者」

   analogies「類似したもの」

19 **specific examples**「具体例」

20 **their underlying ideas**「それらの根底にある考え」

21 **An economic issue**「経済問題」2018（平成 30）年 7 月 17 日、日本と EU は経済連携協定（EPA）に署名した。発効後は世界の国内総生産（GDP）の約 3 割、貿易の約 4 割を占める最大級の自由経済圏の誕生。

   inflation「インフレ」インフレーション。通貨の供給が需要を上回り、通貨価値の下落、物価の上昇を招くこと。

23 **the family budget**「家計」

24 **his contributions to humanitarian causes**「人道的な運動への彼の貢献」

25 **the victims**「被災者」

   the 2011 Great East Japan Earthquake「2011 の年東日本大震災」2011（平成 23）年 3 月 11 日、東北地方沖に発生したマグニチュード 9.0 の地震とそれに伴う津波による災害。

26 **the disaster**「災害」山梨県・カニヤのソフト乾パンは新案フィルム（カニヤバリヤ）を使用しているので 5 年間の保存が可能。災害時に備えた防災食として非常に評価が高い。カニヤ　HP http:www.yin.or.jp/user/kaniya/

27 **console**「慰めを与える」

   victim relief「被災者救済」

28 **Megumi Yokota**「横田めぐみ」1964（昭和 39）年愛知県生まれ。1976（昭和 51）年、家族と共に新潟県に転居。1977（昭和 52）年 11 月、中学校からの帰宅途中に失踪。後に北朝鮮工作員に拉致されたと判明。

   home「居住地」

29 **abduction by North Korea**「北朝鮮による拉致」1970 〜 80 年代に北朝鮮の工作員が多数の日本人を拉致した。

33 **young people**「若者」従来の 20 歳という成人年齢を 18 歳に変更する改正民法が 2022 年 4 月 1 日より施行。1 人で携帯電話や車を購入したり、親の同意なくローンを組んだり、性別変更の申し立てをしたり、1 人で民事裁判を起こすことができるようになるが、飲酒、喫煙、競馬、競輪、養子をとること等は 20 歳以上からで変わらない。

34 **to exercise their right to vote**「投票権を行使するように」

   is your age「みなさんの時代です」

35 **go to the polls**「投票に行く」

36 **meet**「満たす」

Exercise 2-1: COMPREHENSION QUESTIONS

1. What most distinguishes Akira Ikegami's career?
   (A) His ability to tell interesting stories
   (B) The length of time he spent at NHK
   (C) His ability to communicate clearly
   (D) His distinctive style of speaking

2. How did Ikegami learn the principles of clear communication?
   (A) He studied communications in college.
   (B) They came naturally to him.
   (C) He acquired the skill as a reporter for children.
   (D) He picked them up while working as a "boss."

3. What has Ikegami been doing since leaving NHK in 2005?
   (A) He has been searching for his life's work.
   (B) He has been hosting a special news show for children.
   (C) He is enjoying his retirement.
   (D) He has been writing and lecturing and pursuing humanitarian interests.

4. What is one of his techniques for clear communication?
   (A) Understanding the underlying concepts
   (B) Using a highly technical vocabulary
   (C) Telling audiences to be better listeners
   (D) Speaking to adults as if they were children

5. Which of these is NOT among Ikegami's humanitarian efforts?
   (A) Consoling victims of the Great East Japan Earthquake
   (B) Fighting inflation
   (C) Trying to solve the North Korean abduction problem
   (D) Encouraging active participation by young people in government

Grammar Review

Tense
（時制）

1. 現在形　〈動詞の現在形〉一般動詞は主語が 3 人称単数（he/she/it）の時は〜 s/es。

① 日常的な行為　My grandmother **gets** up early even on Sundays.

② 一般的事実　Australia's capital **is** Canberra, not Sydney.

2. 過去形　〈動詞の過去形〉一般動詞は〜 ed/ 不規則変化。

① 過去の行為　Ikegami **began** his career as a reporter at NHK in 1973.

② 過去の事実　Christopher Columbus **was not** Spanish.

3. 未来形　〈will + 動詞の原形〉

① 単純未来　That **will do** the trick.

② 意志未来　I **will not/won't lend** you any more money.

4. 現在進行形　〈am/is/are + 〜 ing〉

① 現在行われている行為　I **am looking** for a post office.

② 現在の一時的状態　Look at Anita. She **is wearing** a gorgeous dress.

③ 近未来の予定　**Are** you **leaving** tomorrow?

5. 過去進行形　〈was/were + 〜 ing〉

① 過去に行われていた行為　Taro **was eating** at a sushi restaurant.

② 過去の一時的状態　I **was not living** in Japan last fall.

6. 未来進行形　〈will + be + 〜 ing〉

　　未来に行なわれている行為　We **will be taking** an exam this time tomorrow.

7. 現在完了形　〈have/has + 過去分詞〉過去の行為が現在に関係している。

① 完了・結果　**Have** you **eaten** lunch yet?

② 経験　I **have never been** to the Philippines.

③ 継続　He **has made** clear communication his life's work.

④ 現在完了進行形（継続）　They **have been singing** karaoke for six hours.

8. 過去完了形　〈had + 過去分詞〉過去より前の行為が過去に関係している。

① 完了・結果　He **had not found** a good job by then.

② 経験　**Had** you **met** Mr. Green before that?

③ 継続　We **had lived** in Naha for 10 years when we moved away last month.

④ 過去完了進行形（継続）　They **had been working** for twelve hours when they called it a day.

9. 未来完了形　〈will + have + 過去分詞〉未来より前の行為が未来に関係している。

① 完了・結果　Ben **will not have made** up his mind by tomorrow.

② 経験　Miho **will have grown** up after studying abroad.

③ 継続　Mr. Simon **will have taught** at this school for 20 years next year.

④ 未来完了進行形（継続）　It **will have been snowing** for a week if it doesn't let up tomorrow.

Exercise 2-2: Grammar Exercise

（　　）の中の動詞を適切な形に変えて、＿＿＿＿＿＿に書き入れなさい。

1. The DVD is still not available, so you will have to wait until it _____ next month. (release)

2. He _____ to the hotel without making a reservation, so he wasn't able to get a room. (go)

3. I think Justin _____ next year's Grammy Award for Best Pop Vocalist. (win)

4. Tom _____ his car when I called on him this morning. (wash)

5. I _____ this movie twice before, but I would like to see it again. (see)

6. She _____ for the exam tomorrow all day today. (study)

7. I later realized that I _____ my cell phone on the train. (leave)

Exercise 2-3: Listening Practice

CD を聞いて空欄に正しい語を入れなさい。

In 1977, Megumi Yokota suddenly (1. _____) from her home, a victim of abduction by North Korea. In 2017, Akira Ikegami met Megumi's mother, (2. _____) her hope and encouragement, and spoke out on behalf of her and others in a similar situation: "The government must (3. _____) with the U.S. and the United Nations to solve these tragic cases."

Ikegami (4. _____) young people to become active citizens and, especially, to exercise their right to vote. "The 21st century is your age," he recently told them. "If you go to the polls, our leaders will hear your voices, and (5. _____) policies that meet your needs."

CHAPTER 3
Kakuei Tanaka

田中角栄

Kakuei Tanaka, who passed away in 1993, was one of the most powerful figures in postwar Japanese politics. Always controversial, Tanaka dramatically altered the country's political climate. Using his considerable charisma and pragmatic leadership style, he moved the government beyond ideological squabbles to open debate of the issues.

There has recently been a resurgence of interest in Tanaka. Topping the best-seller lists in 2016 was a biography entitled *Tensai* (*Genius*). The author was none other than former Tokyo Governor, Shintaro Ishihara. When Tanaka was active, Ishihara often criticized Tanaka and his policies. But the years have apparently tempered Ishihara's views. In his book he lauds Tanaka's accomplishments, comparing him favorably to the 16th-century general, Nobunaga Oda, a brilliant strategist. And Ishihara is not by any means alone in expressing admiration for Tanaka's foresight and ability to get things done.

15 Tanaka's fascinating rags-to-riches story began in 1918 when he was born in a remote village in Niigata Prefecture near the Sea of Japan. At age 15, he began working in construction; by age 18, he had already set up his first construction company. And he was barely 25 when, after a stint in the army, Tanaka saw his company ranked among Japan's top 50 construction 20 outfits.

In 1947, Tanaka entered politics, winning a seat in the House of Representatives, where he served for 43 years, until 1990. In 1957, he headed the Ministry of Posts and Communications, drawing up legislation that still governs emerging media and technology. In 1962, 25 he served as Finance Minister, and in 1971, Tanaka also led the Ministry of International Trade and Industry (MITI). Overseeing one of the most prosperous periods in Japanese economic history, he laid the foundation for the nation's current infrastructure: Shinkansen networks, highway grids, ports and harbors, Tsukuba Science City, Narita Airport, and tunnels 30 to Hokkaido. All of these exist today thanks to Tanaka's political acumen and far-sightedness.

As Japan's prime minister (1972-1974), Tanaka was a popular leader who accomplished a great deal, including the restoration of relations with China. After resigning as prime minster, Tanaka became known as 35 the Liberal Democratic Party's (LDP) "kingmaker," and wielded great influence in shaping Japan's future. His aggressiveness led some to dub him a "Computerized bulldozer." Today, once again, his abilities and achievements continue to win him high praise, with some even saying, "It is Kakuei Tanaka who built Japan's present framework."

Notes

21 *Kakuei Tanaka* 「田中角栄」政治家。1918（大正 7）年〜 1993（平成 5）年。新潟県生まれ。自由民主党等に所属。衆議院議員（16 期）。郵政大臣、大蔵大臣、自民党幹事長、通商産業大臣を歴任後、内閣総理大臣（1972 〜 74）を務めた。1972（昭和 47）年、日中国交正常化を実現。著書『日本列島改造論』で田中角栄ブームが起きた。田中自身の議員立法 33 本。揮発油税を財源に道路を集中整備した「道路整備費の財源等に関する臨時措置法」を始め、次々と編み出す議員立法で国土開発を推し進めた。
2 **powerful figures** 「権力を持った人物」

3 **political climate**「政治的風潮」

4 **charisma**「カリスマ性」人を引き付ける魅力。

5 **ideological squabbles**「イデオロギー的な論争」主義、信条に基づく論争。

6 **There has recently been a resurgence of interest in**「最近〜への関心が再び高まってきた」
  Topping the best-seller lists「ベストセラーリストのトップになったのは」

7 *Tensai* (*Genius*)「『天才』」石原慎太郎の著書。幻冬舎、2016（平成 28）年。

8 **was none other than**「他でもない〜である」
  former Tokyo Governor「元東京都知事」
  Shintaro Ishihara「石原慎太郎」作家、政治家。1932（昭和 7）年兵庫県生まれ。

10 **have apparently tempered Ishihara's views**「石原の見方を和らげたようである」

11 **comparing**「比肩している」

12 **Nobunaga Oda**「織田信長」戦国武将。1534（天文 3）年〜 1582（天正 10）年。

22 13 **foresight and ability to get things done**「先見性と実行力」田中角栄は政治家のリーダーとして求められる資質（人間力、構想力、決断力、実行力、統率力、交渉力、説得力）をすべて持ち合わせた稀に見る傑出した人物と評されている。

15 **rags-to-riches story**「立身出世物語」

16 **the Sea of Japan**「日本海」

19 **ranked among Japan's top 50 construction outfits**「日本の建設会社上位 50 社のうちに数えられたのを」

21 **seat**「議席」
  the House of Representatives「衆議院」

23 **headed**「〜のトップになった」
  the Ministry of Posts and Communications「郵政省」現在の総務省。
  drawing up legislation「法律を起案した」

25 **Finance Minister**「大蔵大臣」現在の財務大臣。
  the Ministry of International Trade and Industry (MITI)「通商産業省（通産省）」2001（平成 13）年、経済産業省に改称。

26 **Overseeing**「〜を俯瞰しながら」

27 **laid the foundation for**「〜の基礎を築いた」

28 **infrastructure**「インフラ」インフラストラクチャー。エネルギー、交通、通信などの社会経済基盤。
  Shinkansen networks, highway grids, ports and harbors「新幹線網、高速道路網、港湾」

29 **Tsukuba Science City**「筑波研究学園都市」茨城県つくば市にある研究学園地区。
  Narita Airport「成田空港」成田国際空港。千葉県成田市にある。1978（昭和 53）年開港。
  tunnels to Hokkaido「北海道へのトンネル」青函トンネル。1988（昭和 63）年開通。

30 **political acumen and far-sightedness**「政治的洞察力と先見性」

33 **including the restoration of relations with China**「中国との国交回復を含む」1972（昭和 47）年、日中国交正常化。

35 **the Liberal Democratic Party's (LDP)**「自由民主党（自民党）の」1955（昭和 30）年結党。
  "kingmaker,"「キングメーカー」リーダー選任に影響力を持つ人。

36 **His aggressiveness**「彼の積極的な行動力」

37 **a "Computerized bulldozer"**「「コンピューター付きブルドーザー」」田中の頭脳と行動力を賞賛した比喩表現。

39 **Japan's present framework**「現在の日本の骨組み」

Exercise 3-1: COMPREHENSION QUESTIONS

1. Based on the information in the reading, which of these best describes Tanaka?
   (A) Sly and mysterious
   (B) Cool and aloof
   (C) Quiet and self-conscious
   (D) Determined and energetic

2. How has Ishihara changed his view of Tanaka?
   (A) His view has not changed: he always admired Tanaka.
   (B) He believes that Tanaka's accomplishments have been misjudged.
   (C) He once disapproved of him, but now respects him.
   (D) He once approved of him, but now holds him in contempt.

3. All of these statements are true EXCEPT...
   (A) Tanaka went to work when he was a teenager.
   (B) He has been compared to a bulldozer.
   (C) He refused to serve in the military.
   (D) He rose quickly to leadership positions in Japanese politics.

4. What was one of Tanaka's greatest accomplishments?
   (A) Restoring peace after World War II
   (B) Planning the nation's infrastructure
   (C) Winning ideological squabbles
   (D) Writing his autobiography

5. What does the resurgence of interest in Tanaka say about him?
   (A) That he could have accomplished much more
   (B) That he saw himself as a king
   (C) That he should have restored relations with China
   (D) That he was an influential and powerful leader

Grammar Review

Auxiliary Verb
（助動詞）

助動詞
助動詞は〈助動詞＋動詞の原形〉の形を取り、動詞に様々な意味を付け加える。

様々な助動詞

1. will

① 単純未来　Wait patiently. Things **will** go your way.

② 意志未来（依頼）　**Will** you please play the guitar in another room?

③ 推量　These bagels are good. You **will** like them.

2. would　（will の過去形）

① 過去から見た未来　Amy promised me that she **would** not tell my secret to anyone.

② 過去の習慣　My father **would** often take me to Disneyland.

③ 丁寧な依頼　**Would** you spare a little time for me?

3. shall

相手の意思を尋ねる　**Shall** I open the window?

4. should

① 必要　You **should** be more careful when you drive.

② 推量　She took an early plane, so she **should** be in Boston now.

5. used to

過去の習慣　Fred **used to** make a lot of mistakes, but now he knows his job very well.

6. can　（過去形は could）

① 能力・可能　Even smart people **can** make mistakes.

② 許可　Okay, you **can** take five.

③ 依頼　**Can/Could** you bring me an extra plate?

④ 推量　That **can** be true.

7. be able to

能力＋実行　Miwa **was able to** make a speech in English with no mistakes.

8. may　（過去形は might）

① 許可　**May** I ask you some personal questions?

② 推量　This hurricane **may/might** hit Miami.

③ 提案　You **might** want to see a doctor.

④ 禁止　You **may not** take pictures in this museum.

9. must

① 義務　You **must** pay the toll before you enter the highway.

② 推薦　If you go to Japan in summer, you **must** see the firework displays.

③ 確信　Ken's wife passed away. He **must** be very sad.

④ 禁止　You **must not** throw waste away on the street.

10. have to

必要　I **have to** take this book back to the library today.

Exercise 3-2: Grammar Exercise

次の各文の空欄に最もふさわしい語を(A)～(D)の中から選びなさい。

1. The student solved the difficult question quickly. He (   ) be very smart.
   (A) had better   (B) must   (C) ought   (D) would

2. "Have you seen Sam?" "No, but he (   ) be in the cafeteria."
   (A) may   (B) ought   (C) can   (D) would

3. She asked me whether she (   ) travel alone or go as part of a group.
   (A) shall   (B) should   (C) will   (D) would

4. My flight has already departed. I (   ) have left home earlier.
   (A) must   (B) ought   (C) should   (D) used

5. My grandfather (   ) to go jogging before breakfast.
   (A) can   (B) may   (C) should   (D) used

6. She is more polite than anybody else. She (   ) never say such a thing.
   (A) would   (B) may   (C) can   (D) shall

7. Why the boss (   ) have rejected my proposal is a mystery to me.
   (A) shall   (B) must   (C) would   (D) will

Exercise 3-3: Structure and Idiomatic Expression

次の各文のかっこの中から最も適切な語を選びなさい。

1. I read that my favorite author suddenly passed (away / by) last week. What a shame!

2. People often compare life (to / with) a stage.

3. The Constitution of Japan was drawn (as / up) in 1946.

4. Many ski resorts opened early thanks (for / to) a big snow in October.

5. The young actor is known (as / to) a hero among young people for his humanitarian work.

26

CHAPTER 4
Barack Obama's Hiroshima Speech

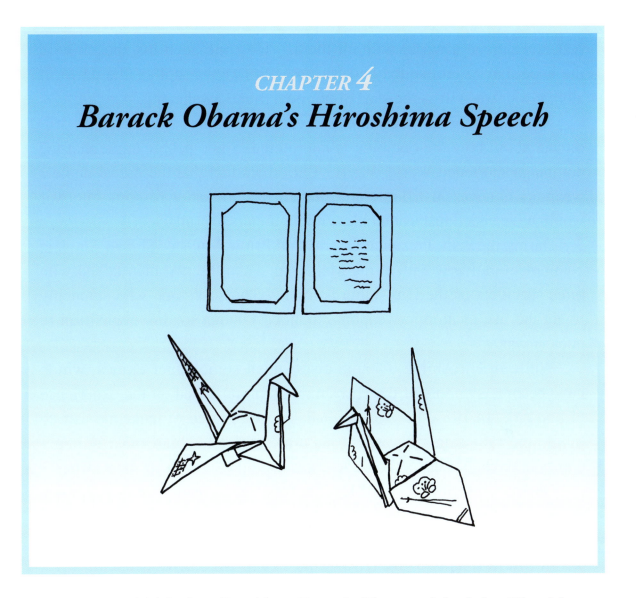

In May 2016, then-President Barack Obama visited the Hiroshima Peace Memorial Park. In the speech he gave on that day, he memorialized those who had died there in the 1945 nuclear bombing of Hiroshima and pleaded for a nuclear-free future: "We come to mourn the dead, including over a hundred thousand Japanese men, women, and children, thousands of Koreans, and a dozen Americans held prisoner." Obama stressed the importance of remembering that day in 1945 when "death fell from the sky and the world was changed." He described that day as a demonstration "that mankind possessed the means to destroy itself."

Obama, who has long supported global nuclear disarmament, also urged the world to change: "But among those nations like my own that hold nuclear stockpiles, we must have the courage to escape the logic of

fear and pursue a world without them." He concluded his speech with the hope that "...Hiroshima and Nagasaki are known not as 'the dawn of
15 atomic warfare,' but as the start of our own moral awakening."

Although Obama's sentiments were well received, differences still remain about how the bombing is interpreted. Some people argue that the bombings shortened World War II. But others feel that the use of nuclear weapons is never justifiable and that for a number of reasons, the war
20 would have ended just as quickly without the nuclear attack.

During the visit, President Obama and Prime Minister Shinzo Abe laid a commemorative wreath at the Memorial. Then the two men talked with three survivors of the Hiroshima bombing. The survivors, who staunchly reject the use of atomic weapons, thanked Obama for his opposition to
25 nuclear war.

While in Hiroshima, Obama also folded some paper cranes, which have become symbols of the Hiroshima bombing based on the experience of one girl. In 1955, 12-year-old Sadako Sasaki died of leukemia caused by atomic radiation. She spent her time in the hospital making paper
30 cranes in the belief that a thousand cranes could make wishes come true.

Obama's inscription—his Message for Peace—read: "We have known the agony of war. Let us now find the courage, together, to spread peace, and pursue a world without nuclear weapons."

In a letter sent to the Hiroshima Peace Memorial Museum after
35 visiting Hiroshima, Obama wrote: "So long as more people take the time to understand the past and embrace compassion, I am confident a brighter, more peaceful future lies ahead."

Notes

27 ***Barack Obama's Hiroshima Speech*** 「バラク・オバマヒロシマスピーチ」2016（平成28）年5月27日、アメリカのオバマ大統領が現職大統領として初めて広島市を訪問した際、核兵器廃絶を訴えて行なったスピーチ。
　1 **then-President**「当時の大統領」
　　Barack Obama「バラク・オバマ」第44代アメリカ合衆国大統領（2009年～2017年）。1961年ハワイ州生まれ。2009（平成19）年ノーベル平和賞受賞。
　　the Hiroshima Peace Memorial Park「広島平和記念公園」1954（昭和29）年、広島市中区に完成。原爆投下による犠牲者の慰霊碑、平和記念資料館等がある。
　2 **memorialized**「追悼した」

3 **the 1945 nuclear bombing of Hiroshima**「1945 年の広島への原爆投下」1945（昭和 20）年 8 月 6 日、原子爆弾が広島に投下された。

4 **pleaded for**「～を嘆願して言った」

a nuclear-free future「核のない未来」

"We come to mourn the dead, including over a hundred thousand Japanese men, women, and children, thousands of Koreans, and a dozen Americans held prisoner."「「私たちは 10 万人を超す日本の男女、そして子供たち、何千人もの朝鮮人、そして 10 数人の米国人捕虜を含む死者を悼むために訪れたのです。」」

7 **"death fell from the sky and the world was changed"**「「死が空から降り、世界が変わってしまった」」

8 **demonstration**「証明」

"that mankind possessed the means to destroy itself"「「人類が自らを破滅させる手段を手に入れた」」

10 **global nuclear disarmament**「世界的な核軍縮」

11 **"But among those nations like my own that hold nuclear stockpiles, we must have the courage to escape the logic of fear and pursue a world without them."**「「しかし、私自身の国のように核の備蓄を保有する国々の間では、私たちは恐怖の論理にとらわれず、核なき世界を追求する勇気を持たなければなりません。」」

14 **"... Hiroshima and Nagasaki are known not as 'the dawn of atomic warfare,' but as the start of our own moral awakening."**「「広島と長崎が〈核戦争の夜明け〉ではなく、私たちが道徳的に目覚めることの始まりとして知られる」」

17 **the bombing**「原爆投下」

21 **Prime Minister Shinzo Abe**「安倍晋三首相」1954（昭和 29）年東京都生まれ。成蹊大学卒。自由民主党幹事長、官房長官、内閣総理大臣等を歴任。

22 **a commemorative wreath**「追悼の花輪」

26 **paper cranes**「折り鶴」

28 **Sadako Sasaki**「佐々木禎子」1943（昭和 18）年〜 1955（昭和 30）年。広島県生まれ。2 歳で被爆。11 歳で白血病を発病し、翌年死去。入院中、回復の願いを込めて折り鶴を折り続けた。

leukemia「白血病」血液がん。

30 **a thousand cranes could make wishes come true**「千羽鶴が願いを叶えてくれる」

31 **inscription**「芳名録」

Message for Peace「平和へのメッセージ」広島平和記念公園にある平和記念資料館の来館者記帳メッセージ。

read「書かれていた」

"We have known the agony of war. Let us now find the courage, together, to spread peace, and pursue a world without nuclear weapons."「「私たちは戦争の苦しみを経験しました。今こそ共に平和を広め、核兵器のない世界を追求する勇気を見出しましょう。」」

34 **the Hiroshima Peace Memorial Museum**「広島平和記念資料館」原爆資料館。

35 **"So long as more people take the time to understand the past and embrace compassion, I am confident a brighter, more peaceful future lies ahead."**「「より多くの人々が時間をかけて過去を理解し、互いを思いやる心を持つ限り、前途にはより明るく、より平和な未来があると、私は確信しています。」」

Exercise 4-1: COMPREHENSION QUESTIONS

1. Why was President Obama visiting Hiroshima?
   (A) To attend an important summit meeting
   (B) To finish his tour of major Asian countries
   (C) To introduce himself to Prime Minister Abe
   (D) To pay tribute to those who died in the 1945 nuclear bombing

2. What did Obama say Hiroshima should remind the world of?
   (A) The need for moral awareness
   (B) The terrible power of nuclear bombs
   (C) The horrors of war
   (D) The will to survive disasters

3. What opinion did the Japanese survivors and Obama seem to share?
   (A) The nuclear bombings ended the Second World War quickly.
   (B) Nuclear stockpiles are difficult to reduce.
   (C) The world would be better off without nuclear weapons.
   (D) Laying a wreath at the memorial was a nice gesture.

4. Why did Obama fold some paper cranes?
   (A) The cranes are a Japanese icon.
   (B) Paper cranes are symbols of the Hiroshima attack.
   (C) Prime Minister Abe urged him to try it.
   (D) He wanted to show his respect for Japanese tradition.

5. What did Obama do after his Hiroshima visit?
   (A) He wrote an inscription and sent it back to the memorial.
   (B) He gave a speech upon arriving back home in the U.S.
   (C) He sent a letter to Hiroshima expressing hope for a better future.
   (D) He discussed Japan-U.S. relations with Prime Minister Abe.

Grammar Review

Noun and Pronoun
（名詞・代名詞）

名詞

１．可算名詞　会話や文章で初めて出る時、通常、a /an ～ , ～ s/es の形を取る。

① 普通名詞　ある種類の事物の名前。

We went on **a picnic** in **a park** yesterday. There were a lot of **pansies** there.

I wrote **an essay** in English. I hope there aren't too many **mistakes**.

② 集合名詞　同じ種類の人や物の集まりの名前。

Our school has 15 **classes**, and my **class** has 35 students.

Every member of this plane's **crew** is well trained.

２．不可算名詞　会話や文章で初めて出る時、通常、a/an, s/es は付かない。

① 物質名詞　天然の物質やそれを素材にした製品の名前。雑多な物の集まりの名前。

Can I get a carton of **milk** and a pound of **ham**?

Pete moved into a new house, so he needs to buy some **furniture**.

② 抽象名詞　情報、観念、感情、状態などの事柄の名前。

This website has a lot of useful **information** about **fitness**.

We must have the **courage** to escape the **logic** of **fear**.

③ 固有名詞　特定の人、土地、事物などの名前。大文字で始める。

In **May** 2016, then-President **Barack Obama** visited the **Hiroshima Peace Memorial Park**.

Some people argue that the bombings shortened **World War II**.

④ 不可算名詞の可算名詞への転用

I'd like **one** large **latte**.　（物質名詞→普通名詞）

Thank you for all your **kindnesses**.　（抽象名詞→普通名詞）

There is a phone call from **a Ms. Smith**.　（固有名詞→普通名詞）

Akira drives **a Toyota**.　（固有名詞→普通名詞）

代名詞

１．人称代名詞　名詞を言い換えたもの。I, we, you, he, she, it, they。格変化がある。

Her bag and **mine** look alike, so **we** sometimes mix **them** up.

She found a dress that suited **her** perfectly. **She** said to **herself**, "It's **my** lucky day."

２．指示代名詞　特定の人、事物を表す。this, that, these, those など。

Are you going to eat up all **these** dishes? **That** sounds like too much.

３．不定代名詞　不特定の人、事物を表す。one, some, any, all, another, other, someone, anyone, everyone, no one, something, anything, everything, nothing など。

I'm looking for a shirt, but I don't like this **one**. Could you show me **some others**?

４．疑問代名詞　疑問を表し、主語、目的語などになる。what, which, who, whose。

Who usually makes breakfast?　（主語）

What do you usually have for breakfast?　（目的語）

Exercise 4-2: Grammar Exercise

次の各文の空欄に最もふさわしい語を(A)〜(D)の中から選びなさい。

1. We'd better hurry up. There is only (   ) time left before the school bus arrives.
   (A) few   (B) a few   (C) little   (D) a little

2. I have to go to New York on a business trip next week. I need (   ) about hotels.
   (A) an information   (B) many informations
   (C) some information   (D) some informations

3. This jacket doesn't suit me. Could you show me (   )?
   (A) another   (B) either   (C) other   (D) other one

4. I ran into a friend of (   ) at the movie theater last night.
   (A) I   (B) my   (C) me   (D) mine

5. Chopsticks made of wood are more expensive than (   ) made of plastic.
   (A) one   (B) which   (C) that   (D) those

Exercise 4-3: Vocabulary Build-up

左の単語と最も近い意味を持つものを右の単語から選びなさい。

1. conclude   (A) war
2. mourn   (B) finish
3. pursue   (C) diffuse
4. surrender   (D) lament
5. conflict   (E) bravery
6. describe   (F) refuse
7. reject   (G) seek
8. courage   (H) express
9. agony   (I) pain
10. spread   (J) yield

CHAPTER 5
The Internet of Things (IoT)

The Internet of Things (IoT) is a digital phenomenon that promises to make our lives more efficient and comfortable. Simply put, the IoT is the vast network of devices connected to the Internet. This includes smartphones and tablets and almost anything with a sensor on or in it —cars, machines in production plants, jet engines, oil drills, wearable devices, and many more. These "things" collect and exchange data.

We can benefit from the IoT in a number of ways. For example, we can remotely control a "smart" home—that is, one in which most of the house's equipment is connected to the Internet. Using a smartphone, we can use apps to raise or lower the temperature in the house, turn lights on or off, or even start the coffee maker. A wearable fitness tracker can measure our daily physical activities, food intake, and sleep patterns. Then it sends the data to a smartphone, where it is stored. In turn, based on the data, the smartphone can offer personalized coaching advice.

15   The IoT offers many possibilities in many fields ranging from manufacturing to medicine. Cars, for instance, can alert the driver when the tire pressure is low. Been involved in an accident? Some IoT-equipped cars can get an ambulance to the scene faster than a phone call. Production lines in factories can be sped up or slowed down automatically. In retail, 20 sensors tally sales and alert management when it is time to order more stock. In agriculture, healthcare, public transportation, and almost every other field, the IoT is hard at work.

    Machine-to-machine (M2M) communication is enabled through sensors, data storage, and data analytics. A sensor gathers raw data such 25 as the number of cars on the road at any given moment. This information is then sent to cloud computing, a special part of the Internet that stores shared online data. Next, cloud-based applications aggregate and analyze the data, combining input from a multitude of sensors. Finally, once the data is interpreted, the analysis can be transmitted to the original 30 "machines." Sensors in stoplights, say, can collect data about the number of vehicles passing through an intersection. Then, as soon as the data is analyzed in the cloud, the traffic signal can change to regulate the traffic flow.

    By one estimate, there will be over 50 billion connected devices in 35 the world by 2020. Perhaps the greatest concern is security, keeping information safe in our age of connectivity.

Notes

33   ***The Internet of Things (IoT)*** 「モノのインターネット（IoT）」家電や自動車、設備などのあらゆるモノをインターネットに接続して、相互に情報をやりとりしたり、遠隔操作したりできる仕組み。
   1 **a digital phenomenon** 「デジタル現象」デジタルテクノロジーによる大量、高速通信の利点が発揮された社会現象。
   2 **Simply put** 「簡単に言えば」
   4 **almost anything with a sensor on or in it** 「センサーの付いたほとんどのモノ」
   5 **oil drills** 「オイルドリル」石油掘削装置。
     wearable devices 「ウェアラブルデバイス」超小型コンピューターチップを内蔵した眼鏡のような身につけることのできるモノ。
   6 **exchange** 「やり取りする」
   8 **"smart" home** 「「スマート」ホーム」家電製品や情報機器等をインターネットを通じて一括して管

理、利用できる住宅。

9 **smartphone**「スマートフォン；スマホ」

10 **apps**「アプリ」アプリケーション。application programs の略語。

11 **fitness tracker**「フィットネストラッカー」体組成、運動量、心拍数、カロリー摂取等を測定、記録する健康管理機器。

12 **physical activities**「身体運動」
　　food intake「食物摂取」

13 **In turn**「折り返し」

14 **personalized coaching advice**「個別の指導アドバイス」

15 **offers**「もたらしている」

16 **manufacturing**「製造業」

17 **the tire pressure**「タイヤの空気圧」

18 **ambulance**「救急車」
　　Production lines「生産ライン」

20 **management**「経営者」

21 **public transportation**「公共交通」

22 **is hard at work**「忙しく作動している」

23 **Machine-to-machine (M2M) communication**「マシンツーマシン（M2M）のコミュニケーション」機械同士がインターネット等で接続され、人の手を介さずに、情報交換、相互制御を行うシステム。

25 **at any given moment**「一定の時刻における」

26 **cloud computing**「クラウドコンピューティング」データをインターネット等を通じてサーバーのコンピューターに保存し、利用するシステム。

27 **cloud-based**「クラウドベースの」クラウドコンピューティングに基づいた。

28 **combining input**「入力信号をまとめる」
　　a multitude of「多数の」

29 **the analysis**「分析結果」
　　can be transmitted「送信されることが可能である」

30 **spotlights**「信号」

32 **to regulate the traffic flow**「交通量を調整するために」

34 **By one estimate, there will be over 50 billion connected devices in the world by 2020.**「ある試算では、2020 年までに世界中で 500 億以上の機器が（ネットに）接続されることになるだろう。」

35 **concern**「懸念」
　　security「セキュリティ」安全性。

36 **connectivity**「コネクティビティ」ネット接続。

Exercise 5-1: COMPREHENSION QUESTIONS

1. What does the word "thing" in "Internet of Things" refer to?
   (A) Anything connected to the Internet
   (B) Any type of sensor or detector
   (C) Actual objects in the real world
   (D) More comfortable lives

2. All of these have made connectivity possible EXCEPT...
   (A) An increase in the number of smartphones and tablets
   (B) Faster operating systems
   (C) Cloud-computing
   (D) Wireless access

3. Which of these can be inferred from the information in the reading?
   (A) People who understand technology benefit most from the IoT.
   (B) Industrial applications are IoT's most important uses.
   (C) Anything with an on/off switch can potentially be connected to the IoT.
   (D) IoT offers faster connection to the Internet.

4. What essentially is M2M communication?
   (A) Communication among machines
   (B) Manually-controlled machines
   (C) Communication between humans and machines
   (D) Data collected by machines

5. What happens to data collected by sensors?
   (A) The data is analyzed by remote office workers.
   (B) The sensors send out alarms to hospitals and police.
   (C) The data is hidden in the cloud for increased security.
   (D) Cloud-based apps collect and analyze the data.

36

Grammar Review

Adjective
(形容詞)

形容詞
形容詞は、名詞の修飾語として、また補語として名詞の性質や状態を表す。

形容詞の用法

1. 限定用法
① 名詞の前に置き、それを修飾する。

A **wearable** fitness tracker can measure our **daily physical** activities.

② someone, nothing などの不定代名詞の後に置き、それを修飾する。

There is nothing **wrong**, but there is nothing **new**, either.

③ 限定用法だけで使われる形容詞　drunken, elder, former, only, wooden など。

My father's **elder** brother is this city's **former** mayor.

2. 叙述用法　形容詞が補語（C）として名詞を説明する。
① S + V + C（第 2 文型）で C になる。

Cars can alert the driver when the tire pressure is **low**.

② S + V + O + C（第 5 文型）で C になる。

The Internet of Things makes our lives more **efficient** and **comfortable**.

③ 叙述用法だけで使われる形容詞　afraid, alive, alone, content, glad, sorry など。

I was **glad** to find that I wasn't **alone** in thinking so.

3. 限定用法と叙述用法で意味が異なるもの　certain, ill, late, present, right など。

I want to get out of my **present** rut. （限定用法）

All her relatives were **present** at her wedding. （叙述用法）

数量形容詞

1. 可算名詞と共に使うもの　数詞（one, two…）, many, a few, few, a number of など。

By **one** estimate, there will be over **50 billion** connected devices.

2. 不可算名詞と共に使うもの　much, a little, little, a good/great deal of など。

We had **a good**/**great deal of** work to do, but we didn't have **much** time.

3. 可算名詞、不可算名詞のどちらとも使えるもの　some, any, no, enough, a lot of など。

A lot of cars were parked in the lot, so there was **no** room for me to park.

名詞を修飾する語句の語順　〈数量 + 属性 / 状態など + 国名など + 素材 / 用途など〉

Barbara has **many beautiful Japanese silk** kimonos.

My grandfather has **an old Swiss travel** clock.

Yuji has **three large American vintage** cars.

Exercise 5-2: Grammar Exercise

次の英単語を形容詞の形に変えなさい。

1. comfort   _____
2. expense   _____
3. avail   _____
4. benefit   _____
5. person   _____
6. act   _____
7. production   _____
8. security   _____

Exercise 5-3: Structure and Idiomatic Expression

次の各文の空欄に最もふさわしい語群をボックスの中から選びなさい。

1. The boy spent the whole morning watching the firefighters (   ).

2. (   ) she entered her room, she changed her clothes.

3. Jack (   ) his computer and checked his mail.

4. Our relationship was (   ) mutual respect.

5. Growth in sales is (   ) because of bad weather.

6. Cartoon characters (   ) Mickey Mouse and Snoopy are very popular around the world.

7. We distribute many books to charities, and (   ), they give the books to children.

(A) as soon as   (B) at work   (C) based on   (D) in turn
(E) slowing down   (F) such as   (G) turned on

CHAPTER 6
Fintech

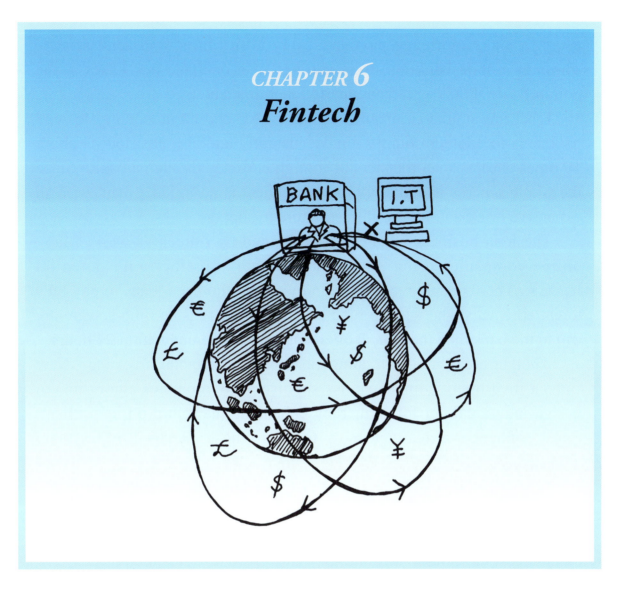

Digital technology is revolutionizing the way people and institutions manage and invest money. This innovative approach is greatly expanding traditional financial services offered by large banks and investment firms. In addition, entrepreneurs are using new software to make many unique services available online to the individual consumer. Financial services of all kinds have become faster, more efficient, and more convenient. The common term for these sweeping changes is "fintech," a word coined from "financial" and "technology." One of fintech's most salient features is the introduction of artificial intelligence (AI) in banking services.

Of all the user-friendly services spawned by fintech, making payments is among the most important. One pioneering company allows consumers to pay vendors online at check-out. The company's system also permits

users to make mortgage payments, pay utility bills, and send money. Through mobile banking, users can get cash or make purchases at the
15 point-of-sale (POS) with their smartphones and tablets.

Emerging online companies enable customers in one country to send payments to another country almost instantly and at a cost that is about 10 times cheaper than transfers of foreign currency through a bank. Since the whole process is digitally processed, there is no "middle man" with an
20 expensive brick-and-mortar infrastructure to support.

The loan business has been transformed by fintech as well. Many online companies bring potential borrowers together with potential lenders. These people range from individuals who need loans to pay bills to entrepreneurs who wish to fund a start-up. There is no time-consuming
25 trip to the bank, and the loan is often approved or denied within 24 hours.

Another area that is attracting customers is financial investing. New fintech investment companies use sophisticated computer algorithms to design individual portfolios thereby enhancing the return on investment. These accounts, in many cases, outperform those managed by financial
30 advisors.

Most banks now offer online services for transactions with other banks and their business clients, even individual customers. Small businesses have found that they can cut costs by accepting digital payments. And consumers, especially millennials who grew up with technology, are
35 rapidly embracing fintech services.

Fintech is one of the business world's most promising industries. Global investment in financial services grew twelvefold in only six years from 2008 to 2014—from 930 million to over 12 billion dollars. The rapid growth of the industry is expected to continue indefinitely, with fintech
40 hubs opening in cities worldwide.

Notes

39 **Fintech** 「フィンテック」 finance または financial と technology を組み合わせた造語。情報技術を利用して、新しい金融サービス、商品を提供するビジネス。
1 **Digital technology** 「デジタルテクノロジー」 コンピューター、インターネットによって、大量の情報を高速で処理する技術。

is revolutionizing「革新しつつある」

2 **This innovative approach**「この革新的な方法」

3 **financial services**「金融サービス」

investment firms「投資会社」証券会社。

4 **entrepreneurs**「起業家」

to make many unique services available online「多くの新しいサービスをオンラインで利用できるようにする」

5 **the individual consumer**「個々の消費者」悪質商法による若者の消費者被害を救済することを主な目的とした消費者契約法の改正法が 2019 年 6 月施行。

7 **sweeping changes**「広範囲に渡る変革」

a word coined from「〜から作られた言葉」

9 **artificial intelligence (AI)**「人工知能（AI）」学習、推論、判断など人間の知能を模したコンピューターシステムを指す。急速に進歩しており、金融、交通、物流、製造などの幅広い分野での効率性向上に加え、医療・介護分野、創薬など開発分野での活用も期待される。囲碁や将棋のプロを負かした AI 棋士や、会話ができる AI スピーカーが話題になった。

10 **user-friendly**「ユーザーに優しい」

11 **is among the most important**「最も重要なことの一つである」

12 **at check-out**「精算時に」

13 **mortgage payments**「ローンの支払い」

utility bills「公共料金」

14 **mobile banking**「モバイルバンキング」携帯電話等を使って、銀行サービスを利用できるシステム。

at the point-of-sale (POS)「店頭（POS）で」

15 **tablets**「タブレット」タッチパネルで操作する小型コンピューター。

18 **transfers of foreign currency**「外貨振込み」

19 **"middle man"**「「中間業者」」

with an expensive brick-and-mortar infrastructure to support「維持するのに費用のかかる店舗インフラを持った」

21 **loan business**「ローンビジネス」貸付業。

has been transformed「転換してきた」

22 **bring potential borrowers together with potential lenders**「お金を借りたいと思っている人たちを、貸してくれそうな人たちと結び付けている」

24 **wish to fund a start-up**「新事業に資金提供したいと考えている」

There is no time-consuming trip to the bank「時間を掛けて銀行に行くこともなく」

26 **financial investing**「金融投資」金融商品の購入などにより、収益を得ること。

27 **algorithms**「アルゴリズム」算出法。

28 **portfolios**「ポートフォリオ」金融商品等の組み合わせ及びその一覧。

the return「収益」

29 **accounts**「取引」

financial advisors「ファイナンシャルアドバイザー」金融アドバイザー。客の投資上のニーズに沿って、情報提供、プラン提案を行う職業。

31 **transactions**「取引」

32 **business clients**「ビジネスクライアント」取引相手の事業者。「ISO9001」は品質マネジメントシステムに関する国際規格のこと。園田税務会計事務所は 2003（平成 15）年に福岡県内・業界第 1号として取得。顧客満足の向上と一貫したサービスの提供を目指している。所在地：福岡県大川市大字津 22-2。所長：園田嘉生。

33 **digital payments**「デジタルでの支払い」インターネットを利用した支払い。

34 **millennials**「ミレニアル世代」1980 年〜 2000 年生まれの人たち。

are rapidly embracing「急速に採用するようになっている」

39 **with fintech hubs opening in cities worldwide**「フィンテックの拠点が世界中の都市に開設され」

Exercise 6-1: COMPREHENSION QUESTIONS

1. What or who primarily is driving the increasing popularity of fintech?
   (A) New technology
   (B) The demand for expanded financial services from entrepreneurs
   (C) Consumers without bank accounts
   (D) Online retailers

2. What are the main benefits of fintech services?
   (A) Decreased staff requirements at banks and investment firms
   (B) Convenience and lower costs
   (C) Loss of trust in traditional banks
   (D) Transparency and open access

3. Which of the following is NOT a fintech service?
   (A) Paying bills
   (B) Making investments in the stock market
   (C) Storing cash in banks
   (D) Lending money to others

4. How are fintech investment companies managed?
   (A) By "millennial" financial advisors
   (B) By free-lance consultants
   (C) By government agencies
   (D) By computer algorithms that analyze market data

5. What does the future hold for fintech?
   (A) It is expected to grow and offer many new opportunities.
   (B) After explosive growth, the industry will soon stabilize.
   (C) It will eventually run out of steam.
   (D) It will be adopted by traditional banks.

Grammar Review

Adverb
（副詞）

副詞

副詞は、動詞、形容詞、他の副詞、節、文などを修飾し、意味を付け加える。

The two cars **nearly** hit each other. （動詞を修飾）

The train left **just** before we got to the station. （節を修飾）

Fortunately, we made it to the airport just in time. （文を修飾）

副詞の形

1. 形容詞に ly を付けるもの　certainly, easily, happily, largely, rapidly, surely など。

Consumers are **rapidly** embracing fintech services.

2. 形容詞と副詞が同形のもの　early, enough, daily, fast, monthly, only, weekly など。

Henry worked so **fast** that he finished the job off **early** in the afternoon.

3. 二つの形があるもの　late/lately, hard/hardly, high/highly, near/nearly など。

The city's new skyscrapers rise **high** above the clouds.

Critics have **highly** acclaimed this novel by a first-time author.

副詞の種類

1. 様態を表す副詞　especially, hard, just, quickly, right, slowly, so, well, wrong など。

Just make sure you brush your teeth before going to bed.

2. 程度を表す副詞　a little, all, almost, hardly, much, nearly, quite, so, very など。

This secondhand PC is **hardly** used. It's **almost** brand-new.

3. 場所、方向を表す副詞　away, back, down, here, in, out, over, there, under など。

It's freezing **out there**, so bundle up.

4. 時を表す副詞　already, before, early, late, now, soon, then, today, yet など。

You showed up **late** again. They've **already** started the meeting.

5. 頻度を表す副詞　always, usually, often, sometimes, never。通常、be 動詞の後、一般動詞の前に置かれるが、文頭や文末に置かれることもある。

I **usually** have coffee with my lunch, but **sometimes** I have tea for a change.

6. 疑問副詞　how, what time, when, where, why。

What time does this supermarket open?

副詞、副詞句の語順

1. 通常、場所、時を表す副詞は単位の小さいものを先に言う。ただし、アメリカ英語では日付は月→日の順で言う。

Abraham Lincoln was born **on February 12, 1809.**

2. 通常、時よりも場所を先に言う。

Abraham Lincoln was born **in Hodgenville, Kentucky, on February 12, 1809.**

Exercise 6-2: Grammar Exercise

次の各文のかっこの中から最も適切な語を選びなさい。

1. Our new CEO cut down on unnecessary running costs and in one year, he had (successful / successfully) turned the business around.

2. You must make sure that things are done (correct / correctly).

3. Whatever it is that you're cooking smells (delicious / deliciously).

4. The dog is wagging its tail (happy / happily).

5. I was really tired last night, so I slept (good / well).

6. The harvest was (poor / poorly) this year because of the drought.

7. I got up earlier than (usual / usually) this morning to watch the Olympic Games on TV.

Exercise 6-3: Listening Practice

CD を聞いて空欄に正しい語を入れなさい。

Most banks now offer online services for transactions with other banks and their business clients, even individual customers. Small businesses have found that they can cut costs by accepting digital payments. And consumers, (1. _____) millennials who grew up with technology, are (2. _____) embracing fintech services. Fintech is one of the business world's most promising industries. Global investment in financial services grew (3. _____) in only six years from 2008 to 2014 from 930 million to over 12 billion dollars. The rapid growth of the industry is expected to continue (4. _____), with fintech hubs opening in cities (5. _____).

CHAPTER 7
Opdivo®

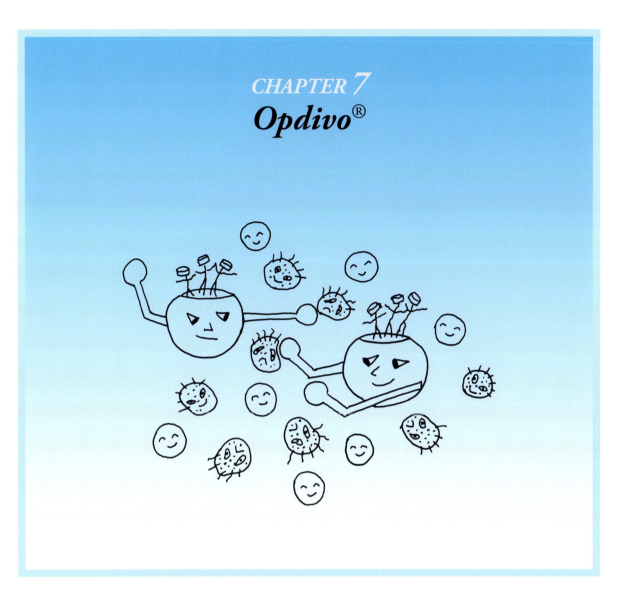

Opdivo is the brand name for a new medication, nivolumab, which offers an innovative immune-based approach to treating cancer. In 2014, in Japan, the drug was approved for treatment of melanoma, and not long thereafter, approval was expanded to include lung and kidney cancer. The new treatment promises to reduce the size of tumors and extend patients' lives.

How does the drug work? The traditional cancer-treatment approach is based on identifying the differences between cancer cells and normal cells and then finding ways to target and kill the cancer cells. Cancer cells generally divide more rapidly than normal cells. Called "targeted therapies" because they address specific differences, all these traditional treatments aim to prevent cancer cells from growing, dividing, or communicating with other cells.

There are three general types of targeted therapies. One focuses on
15 the internal parts of the cells and the way they function. Tiny molecules
are introduced into the cancer cells, where the molecules damage and
ultimately kill them. The second type targets receptors on the outside
of the cancer cells. The third works by cutting off the blood supply and
starving the cancer cells to death.

20 Opdivo, unlike these therapies, is an antibody that strengthens the
immune system. Many cancer cells produce a substance that prevents
T-cells, the body's natural disease fighters, from attacking a tumor.
Opdivo blocks this process, allowing the T-cells to react normally and
attack the cancerous tumor directly. Put another way, Opdivo restores the
25 T-cells' immunological "memory," even when the cells have been treated
previously with other therapies. Because of its unique approach, Opdivo
opens the door to future research into immune therapies for cancer.

Opdivo offers hope for patients who have run out of treatment options.
It is approved for those who cannot be treated surgically or who no longer
30 respond to traditional chemotherapy. Although Opdivo can treat a number
of different types of cancer, it has been most effective for patients with
metastatic melanoma. In one clinical trial, Opdivo produced a one-year
survival rate of 65 percent and a five-year rate of 35 percent.

Like nearly all cancer treatments, Opdivo may cause some serious side
35 effects: fatigue, nausea, and diarrhea, to name the most common. Even so,
most cancer patients opt for the hope that Opdivo offers.

Notes

45 ***Opdivo***®「オプジーボ®」がん治療薬ニボルマブのブランド名。患者自身の免疫機能を高め、がんの予
防、進行抑制、再発及び転移防止に効果がある。2014（平成 26）年、小野薬品工業株式会社（本社：
大阪府大阪市中央区久太郎町 1-8-2）が発売。この新薬を開発した本庶佑（ほんじょ たすく）京都大学
特別教授は、2018（平成 30）年のノーベル医学生理学賞を受賞した。
1 **the brand name**「ブランド名」
 a new medication「新薬」an immune checkpoint inhibitor（免疫チェックポイント阻害剤）がん
 細胞の免疫細胞抑止能力を抑制する働きがある。結果として免疫細胞が本来の力を発揮し、がん
 細胞を攻撃する。
 nivolumab「ニボルマブ」がん治療薬。ブランド名はオプジーボ。
2 **immune-based approach**「免疫に基づく方法」病気への抵抗力を高める療法。

3 **melanoma**「メラノーマ；黒色腫」皮膚の色を作るメラニン形成細胞にがんが発生する病気。

4 **lung and kidney cancer**「肺がん及び腎臓がん」腎臓は尿を作る器官。

5 **promises**「見込みがある」

tumors「腫瘍」

10 **divide**「分裂する」増殖する。

"targeted therapies"「「標的療法」」特定のがん細胞を標的にして、薬物等で攻撃する治療法。

11 **address specific differences**「明確な相違点を的をしぼる」

12 **growing, dividing, or communicating with other cells**「肥大化したり、分裂したり、あるいは他の細胞に感染したりするのを」

46 | 15 **molecules**「分子」

16 **are introduced**「注入される」

17 **receptors**「受容体」

18 **works**「効力を発揮する」

cutting off the blood supply「血液の供給を遮断すること」

19 **starving the cancer cells to death**「がん細胞を餓えさせて壊死させること」

20 **an antibody**「抗体」免疫体。病原体に対して抵抗する体内物質。

the immune system「免疫組織」

22 **T-cells**「T 細胞」骨髄の幹細胞から出される免疫細胞。

the body's natural disease fighters「病気と闘う体の天然物質」

24 **the cancerous tumor**「がん性腫瘍」

the T-cells' immunological "memory,"「T 細胞の免疫学的「記憶」」天然の免疫機能。

27 **immune therapies**「免疫療法」

28 **offers hope**「希望をもたらしている」

have run out of treatment options「治療法の選択肢が尽きてしまった」

29 **cannot be treated surgically**「外科的に治療のできない」

30 **chemotherapy**「化学療法」抗がん剤による治療法。

32 **metastatic melanoma**「転移性メラノーマ（黒色腫）」内臓に転移したメラノーマ（黒色腫）。

In one clinical trial「ある臨床試験で」

produced「もたらした」

33 **survival rate**「生存率」

34 **side effects**「副作用」

35 **to name the most common**「最も一般的なものを挙げれば」

Even so, most cancer patients opt for the hope that Opdivo offers.「それでも、ほとんどのがん患者たちはオプジーボがもたらす希望を選択している。」

Exercise 7-1: COMPREHENSION QUESTIONS

1. Which of these is the most important potential benefit of Opdivo for cancer patients?
    (A) A longer life
    (B) Fewer side effects
    (C) No new cancerous growths
    (D) More T-cells

2. How do traditional targeted therapies work?
    (A) They require surgical removal of cancer cells.
    (B) They strengthen the immune system.
    (C) They act on the cancer cells directly.
    (D) They protect normal cells.

3. Why don't T-cells normally attack cancer cells?
    (A) They act only on normal cells.
    (B) Cancer cells produce a substance that prevents T-cell activity.
    (C) They are reduced in number.
    (D) T-cells are affected by body chemistry.

4. What makes Opdivo such an innovative treatment?
    (A) It is used to strengthen other cancer drugs.
    (B) It eliminates the need for surgery.
    (C) It mimics cancer cells.
    (D) It enables T-cells to attack tumors.

5. What group of patients is Opdivo recommended for?
    (A) Those for whom traditional cancer treatments have failed
    (B) All melanoma patients
    (C) Patients who want to speed up and supplement current cancer treatments
    (D) Patients with any kind of cancerous tumor

Grammar Review

Comparison
（比較）

形容詞、副詞の比較変化

1. 〈-er, -est〉 1 音節語。-er, -le, -ow, -some, -y などで終わる 2 音節語。

long（原級）→ **longer**（比較級）→ **longest**（最上級）

narrow → **narrower** → **narrowest**

2. 〈more 〜 , most 〜〉 -ful, -ish, -ive, -ous などで終わる 2 音節語。3 音節以上の語。

useful（原級）→ **more useful**（比較級）→ **most useful**（最上級）

important → **more important** → **most important**

3. 不規則変化するもの

little（原級）→ **less**（比較級）→ **least**（最上級）

many/much → **more** → **most**

good/well → **better** → **best**

bad/ill → **worse** → **worst**

様々な比較表現

1. 原級を用いた表現

① as + 原級 + as 〜 「〜と同じくらい…」

Mika studies **as hard as** Reika (does).

② less + 原級（+ 名詞）+ than 〜 「〜ほど…でない」

This actor is a little **less talented than** we thought.

2. 比較級を用いた表現

① 比較級 + than 〜 「〜よりも…」

Cancer cells generally divide **more rapidly than** normal cells (do).

② much/far + 比較級 + than 〜 「〜よりもずっと…」

We practice **much/far harder than** they do.

3. 最上級を用いた表現

①（the）+ 最上級（+ 名詞）「最も…」

Opdivo has been **most effective** for patients with metastatic melanoma.

② much/by far + the + 最上級（+ 名詞）「断然…」

Frank is **much/by far the smartest** person in our company.

4. 慣用表現

① 比較級 and 比較級「ますます…」

More and more Japanese are having parties in their homes.

② the + 比較級〜 , the + 比較級… 「〜すればするほど、ますます…」

The more you have, **the more** you want.

Exercise 7-2: Grammar Exercise

かっこ内の語句を並び替えて、日本文に合う英文を作りなさい。

1. 私はひろしほど熱心に英語を勉強してこなかった。
   (as / as / earnest / English / haven't / Hiroshi / I / in / much / studied)

2. 私は兄の半分しかお金を持っていません。
   (as / as / brother / half / have / I / money / much / my / only)

3. 彼女は5人の学生のうちではるかに一番速く走ることができる。
   (by / can / far / fastest / five / of / run / she / students / the / the)

4. 彼はアメリカで最も評価されている歌手である。
   (acclaimed / he / in / is / most / singer / the / the United States)

5. オプジーボは他のものよりも期待のできる治療である。
   (a / hopeful / is / more / Opdivo / others / than / treatment)

Exercise 7-3: Vocabulary Build-up

左の単語と最も反対に近い意味を持つものを右の単語から選びなさい。

1. innovative   (A) artificial
2. expand   (B) demand
3. common   (C) diminish
4. survival   (D) general
5. difference   (E) defense
6. divide   (F) death
7. supply   (G) rare
8. natural   (H) similarity
9. specific   (I) conventional
10. attack   (J) unite

50

CHAPTER 8
Environmental DNA

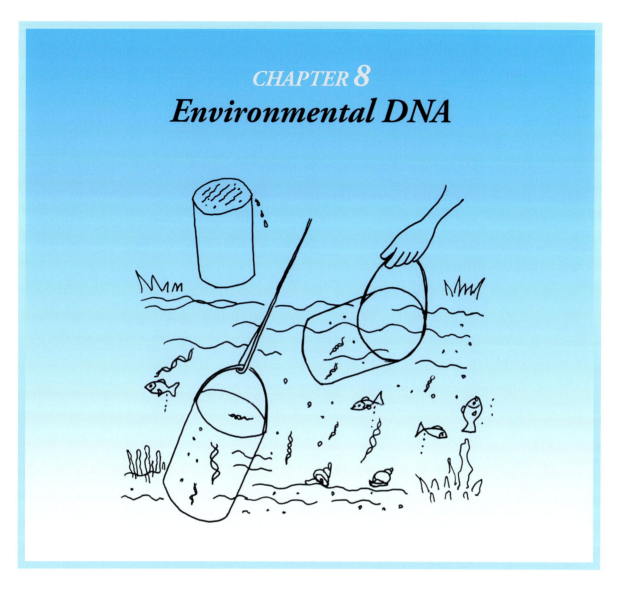

Any ecosystem's biodiversity is an important way to assess its health. The greater the diversity, the more sustainable the ecosystem is. Every species is important to an ecosystem's overall strength. However, to detect or monitor the presence of all species in a particular environment is a major challenge. Fortunately, a new tool for monitoring past and present biodiversity in water is emerging—environmental DNA (eDNA).

Environmental DNA comes from the traces of existence—similar to a genetic fingerprint—that all living creatures scatter in their wake as they pass through life. Fish and other aquatic organisms leave eDNA in lakes or streams. Among eDNA's most common sources are excrement, shed skin cells, and body fluids like blood or urine. All living creatures are identified by simply analyzing the eDNA found in a bucket of water drawn from a lake or stream.

No one knows for sure how long eDNA persists in water. As a general estimate, eDNA lasts only a week or two, but several factors affect its endurance. Because exposure to light and heat tend to destroy eDNA, the ideal environment is dark, and very cold.

Despite eDNA's short persistence in some waters, it still provides an easier, more reliable, and less expensive way to learn more about life in our waterways. In the past, the main technique for identifying various species meant using nets or traps to capture fish, insects, and so on, which were then identified by their appearance.

But this traditional method has some problems. First, catching endangered species is tricky because there are so few individual specimens. Second, even experts cannot identify all species by appearance, especially tiny invertebrates.

In contrast, the analysis of eDNA gives us a quick way to collect more reliable data: to decode the genome of fishes. This analysis may reveal the presence of new species, as well as trends in the population growth or decline of existing species. Another advantage is that eDNA can be detected at very low densities, allowing us to find hidden or rare species.

The biodiversity of the Earth is at risk. More precise understanding of an ecosystem will allow us to conserve and protect its diversity more effectively. New knowledge is essential to slowing environmental decline.

Notes

51 | *Environmental DNA* 「環境 DNA」略称 :eDNA。海、川、湖などに含まれる DNA（遺伝子情報）を分析することで、生息する生物の種類、数などを知ることができる。
1 **ecosystem's** 「生態系の」互いに関係し合って機能する生物と環境の体系。
biodiversity 「生物多様性」生物の種類の豊富さ。
assess 「評価する」環境への影響を評価する。
2 **sustainable** 「環境持続的」
3 **species** 「種」生物の種類。
to detect or monitor 「発見あるいは観察すること」
5 **a new tool** 「新しいツール」新しい手段。
6 **is emerging** 「生まれつつある」
7 **comes from** 「〜から得られる」
the traces of existence 「生存の痕跡」
a genetic fingerprint 「遺伝子的な指紋」
8 **living creatures** 「生き物」

scatter in their wake as they pass through life「一生を過ごしながら、その跡に点々と残す」

9 aquatic organisms「水中生物」

10 excrement「排泄物」ふんなどの排出物。

shed skin cells「脱皮した皮膚細胞」

11 body fluids「体液」魚の体から分泌される粘液など。

are identified「識別される」

12 analyzing「分析すること」

14 persists「残存する」

As a general estimate「大まかに見積もって」

16 exposure to「〜に当たること」

18 persistence「持続性」

some waters「いくらかの水域」

20 waterways「水路」

22 by their appearance「外見によって」

24 endangered species「絶滅危惧種」個体数が絶滅の恐れがあるほど減少している野生生物。

tricky「難しい」

26 tiny invertebrates「微小な無脊椎動物」ゾウリムシ、ミドリムシなど。

28 to decode the genome of fishes「魚のゲノムを解読すること」ゲノムは全遺伝情報。高速で魚のゲノム配列を解読する次世代シークエンサーを使い、多くの種が混在する DNA を同時に解析する技術が確立された。

29 as well as trends in the population growth or decline of existing species「現存する種の個体数の増減の傾向だけでなく」

31 at very low densities「非常に低い濃度で」

32 is at risk「危機的な状態にある」

34 decline「衰退」

Exercise 8-1: COMPREHENSION QUESTIONS

1. How is the health of an ecosystem diagnosed?
   (A) By introducing new species into it
   (B) By assessing its biodiversity
   (C) By capturing different animal species
   (D) By discovering hidden species

2. What is eDNA?
   (A) An organism's genetic code
   (B) The composition of a body of water
   (C) DNA that comes from a single living cell
   (D) DNA from living things that remains in the environment

3. How long can eDNA persist?
   (A) Not as long as regular DNA
   (B) Most likely forever
   (C) No tests for its persistence exist
   (D) Roughly one or two weeks

4. Which of these is a traditional way to evaluate a stream's or lake's biodiversity?
   (A) Observing the life cycle of a particular fish
   (B) Taking samples with a net or a trap
   (C) Testing water quality with special instruments
   (D) Using underwater photography

5. All of these are mentioned as advantages of eDNA testing EXCEPT...
   (A) Lower costs
   (B) More rapid assessment
   (C) Prevention of water pollution
   (D) Discovery of rare species

Grammar Review

Passive Voice
（受動態）

能動態と受動態

1. 能動態　行為の主体を主語にする。動詞は現在形、過去形などになる。

   Many music fans **love** her.

2. 受動態　行為の客体が話題の中心である時、それを主語にする。動詞は〈be + 過去分詞〉。行為の主体は by 〜で表されるが、しばしば省略される。

   She **is loved by** many music fans.

各時制における受動態

1. 現在形　〈am/is/are + 過去分詞〉

   The president **is elected** every four years.

   Public phones **are not used** by many people these days.

2. 過去形　〈was/were + 過去分詞〉

   In the past, fish and insects **were identified** by their appearance.（by は手段を表す。）

   Was this vase really **broken** by Jack?

3. 未来形　〈will + be + 過去分詞〉

   You can trust me. My promise **will be kept**.

   Your theory **will not be accepted** by experts.

4. 進行形　〈be + being + 過去分詞〉

   The cafeteria **is being enlarged** and **redecorated**.

   Is the road ahead **being repaired**?

5. 完了形　〈have/has/had/will have + been + 過去分詞〉

   The debris **had** already **been cleared**.

   The report **has not been submitted** yet.

様々な受動態

1. 助動詞と受動態　〈助動詞 + be + 過去分詞〉

   Environmental DNA **can be detected** at very low densities.

2. 句動詞と受動態　be laughed at, be looked up to, be taken care of など。

   Soseki Natsume **is looked up to** as a great writer.

3. be 動詞以外を使う受動態　get + 過去分詞 , feel + 過去分詞 , look + 過去分詞など。

   I **felt relieved** when I heard that the typhoon had passed.

4. by 〜以外を使う受動態　be based on 〜 , be filled with 〜 , be known to 〜など。

   This movie **is based on** a true story.

5. 〈have + 目的語 + 過去分詞〉「…を〜される」

   He **had** his umbrella **blown** out by the strong wind.

Exercise 8-2: Grammar Exercise

次の各文のかっこの中から最も適切な語を選びなさい。

1. All the teachers should be acquainted (at / with) the school's fire exit routes.
2. The customer is not satisfied (at / with) the way I cut her hair.
3. My eyes quickly became accustomed (for / to) the dark.
4. Mr. Lucas is convinced (of / to) the possibility of life on other planets.
5. The prime minister was disappointed (at / of) having to endure a situation that he couldn't control.
6. The trench was already filled (in / with) stinking brown water.
7. Cheese is made (from / of) milk.

Exercise 8-3: Vocabulary Build-up

次の各語の定義として最もふさわしいものを(A)〜(G)の中から選びなさい。

1. diversity
2. expert
3. ecosystem
4. endurance
5. data
6. identify
7. analysis

(A) careful examination of a substance or other entity to see what it is made of or to understand it
(B) the ability to continue doing something difficult or painful over a long period of time
(C) to recognize something or to discover exactly what its nature or origin is
(D) a person who has a special skill or special knowledge of a subject, gained as a result of training or experience
(E) all the animals and plants in a particular area, and the way in which they are related to each other and to their environment
(F) a range of different people, things, or ideas
(G) information or facts that have been gathered in order to be studied

CHAPTER 9
Camellia

椿の造花

   The camellia is the city flower of Ofunato City in Iwate Prefecture where the Goishi Camellia Museum is located. Some 550 varieties of camellia from 13 countries are on display there. The camellias are grown in the Kesen Area, which consists of Ofunato City, Rikuzen-Takata City, and Sumita Town, and are known as the Kesen Camellia. Because the camellia survived the 2011 Great East Japan Earthquake and tsunami, the flower has become a symbol of hope and an important part of efforts to spur recovery in the region. In fact, Shiseido, the famous cosmetic maker, is continuing to plant camellias to give aid to Ofunato City and to increase the area's seed crops. Shiseido's logo is a camellia blossom. As the Shiseido's president is keen to engage in corporate social responsibility (CSR), the company has been promoting the support of the disaster area.

A flowering plant with red blossoms, the camellia is the source of an oil that can be used in many different ways. Camellia oil, which is
15 extracted from the plant's seeds, is edible and can also be used as a hair treatment. But nowadays it is being used primarily as an ingredient in beauty products such as hand cream, lip balm, and body cream. The oil is rapidly absorbed by the skin, helping it to retain moisture, and has the ability to penetrate the deepest layers of the skin, keeping it soft and
20 smooth.

Residents in the Kesen Area have traditionally handpicked camellia seeds, and, until recently, factories and people in the area produced the camellia's oil for cooking and hair care.

But then some local entrepreneurs, as a possible avenue to revitalize
25 the region and create jobs, saw an opportunity for camellia production for the cosmetics market.

In 2012, a cosmetics company teamed up with a group of female doctors to develop a new hand cream. The new product was launched that year, and other new products were later added, including lip balms. The
30 cosmetics company produced the products, while the doctors advised on texture, scent, and package design.

Sustainable community development is the goal of the camellia oil revival. Achieving the goal means keeping local control of the business and creating local jobs. To this end, the enterprising entrepreneurs decided
35 to develop the market for the camellia products such as Camellia Tea, and in 2017, a new factory was opened near the Kumano Shrine in Ofunato City. The ultimate aim is to expand sales of Kesen Camellia products both in Japan and abroad in the near future.

Notes

57   *Camellia*「つばき」椿。岩手県大船渡市は太平洋沿岸のやぶつばき実取りの北限として知られている。つばきは大船渡市の花。つばき油は椿の種子から採取される植物性油脂。食品、整髪料、化粧品、薬品等に使われる。
写真説明：椿の造花。製作：ふるさと工房 やぶ椿。代表 沼田京子。岩手県大船渡市大船渡町字上山 5-10。
1 **Ofunato City**「大船渡市」演歌シンガーソングライターで知られる大沢桃子が作詞作曲した「椿の咲く港」が評判となっている。大沢桃子：岩手県大船渡市生まれ。HP http://bspro.jp/momoko
Iwate Prefecture「岩手県」

2 **the Goishi Camellia Museum**「世界の椿館・碁石」1997（平成 9）年オープン。世界 13 か国、約 550 種類の椿が展示されている。所在地：岩手県大船渡市末崎町字大浜 280-1。

3 **are on display**「展示されている」
  are grown「栽培されており」

4 **the Kesen Area**「気仙（けせん）地方」岩手県南部の旧気仙郡（現在の大船渡市、陸前高田市、住田町）を指す呼称。
  Rikuzen-Takata City, and Sumita Town「陸前高田市、そして住田町」

5 **the Kesen Camellia**「気仙（けせん）椿」

6 **the 2011 Great East Japan Earthquake and tsunami**「2011 年の東日本大震災と津波」2011（平成 23）年 3 月 11 日、東北地方沖に発生したマグニチュード 9.0 の地震とそれに伴う津波。

7 **efforts to spur recovery**「復興に拍車を掛ける努力」

8 **Shiseido**「資生堂」1872（明治 5）年創業。

10 **logo**「ロゴ」商標、社名などのデザイン化されたもの。
  a camellia blossom「花椿」

11 **is keen to engage in**「〜にかかわることに熱心である」
  corporate social responsibility (CSR)「企業の社会的責任（CSR）」利益の追求だけではなく、従業員、消費者、地域社会、環境などに配慮した企業活動を行うべきとする経営理念。

58 13 **A flowering plant**「顕花植物」花を咲かせる植物。
  the source「採取源」

14 **Camellia oil**「椿油」酔仙（すいせん）酒造株式会社（岩手県大船渡市猪川町字久名畑 136-1）は原料のひとつに椿油を使った美容液「雪っこ オールインワンジェル」を開発。化粧水、乳液、保湿液、美容液、クリームの 5 役を担う優れものとして評価が高い。
  is extracted from「〜から抽出される」

17 **beauty products**「化粧品」
  lip balm「リップクリーム」

18 **helping it to retain moisture**「保湿を助け」

19 **the ability to penetrate the deepest layers of the skin**「皮膚の最深層に浸透する効能」

21 **have traditionally handpicked camellia seeds**「伝統的につばきの実を手で拾い集めてきた」

24 **local entrepreneurs**「地元の起業家たち」
  as a possible avenue to revitalize the region and create jobs「地域を再活性化し、雇用を創出する可能性のある手段として」

27 **a cosmetics company**「ある化粧品会社」ハリウッド株式会社（ハリウッド化粧品）：東京都六本木 6-4-1 ハリウッドビューティプラザ。
  teamed up with「〜と協力した」

28 **was launched**「発売された」

31 **texture**「質感」肌触り。

32 **Sustainable community development**「サステナブル（環境持続可能）な地域発展」

33 **keeping local control of the business**「地元でビジネス管理をすること」

34 **this end**「この目的」
  the enterprising entrepreneurs「チャレンジ精神旺盛な起業家たち」

35 **Camellia Tea**「椿茶」血糖値上昇抑制、体脂肪、中性脂肪の低下等の効能があると言われている。発売元：株式会社バンザイ・ファクトリー。HP https://www.sagar.jp/　株式会社カメリア社中。HP http://came-sha.co.jp/

36 **the Kumano Shrine**「熊野神社」境内にある三面椿は樹齢 1400 年といわれている日本最大・最古のやぶつばき。1969（昭和 44）年、岩手県が天然記念物に指定。2016（平成 28）年、石の碁盤が奉納されて以来、囲碁神社としても知名度を上げている。所在地：岩手県大船渡市末崎町字中森。

Exercise 9-1: COMPREHENSION QUESTIONS

1. Why has the camellia become a symbol of hope?
   (A) It survived the Great East Japan Earthquake and tsunami.
   (B) It is a source of economic prosperity for the region.
   (C) The large, red blossoms have an especially nice scent.
   (D) The plant has many different uses.

2. Where does most camellia oil used in cosmetics come from?
   (A) Foreign producers
   (B) All over Japan
   (C) Newly built farms
   (D) The Kesen Area in Iwate Prefecture

3. Which of these is true?
   (A) Local farms have cut back on production of camellias.
   (B) The costs for oil-extraction are too high to make camellia production profitable.
   (C) The versatility of camellia oil is now being exploited.
   (D) Overseas oils have replaced camellia oil for cooking.

4. What is camellia oil being used for these days?
   (A) As a cooking oil in health-food stores
   (B) As a logo for Shiseido
   (C) In cosmetics products and tea
   (D) As a treatment for skin diseases

5. What are the goals of the camellia revival?
   (A) To preserve tradition in the region
   (B) To provide a source of sustainable development
   (C) To encourage local farmers
   (D) To attract tourists to Iwate Prefecture

Grammar Review

Participle
（分詞）

分詞の形と意味

1. 現在分詞 〈動詞の原形＋ing〉「～する,～している」

   coming, driving, running, playing, sleeping, standing, swimming, walking など。

2. 過去分詞 〈-ed または不規則変化〉①「～された」（他動詞） ②「～した」（自動詞）

   ① broken, covered, lost, written など。 ② drunk, faded, fallen, gone など。

分詞の用法

1. 〈分詞＋名詞〉で分詞が形容詞の働き。単独で用いる時は名詞の前に置く。

   ① 現在分詞 the **coming** spring a **sleeping** baby a **walking** man

   ② 過去分詞 **broken** glass my **lost** wallet **faded** flowers **fallen** leaves

2. 〈名詞＋分詞〉で分詞が形容詞の働き。修飾語等を伴う時は名詞の後に置く。

   ① 現在分詞 the man **standing** over there children **playing** make-believe

   ② 過去分詞 a letter **written** in English days **gone** by

3. S＋V＋C（分詞） go ～ ing, keep ～ ing, stand ～ ing, lie ～ ed, feel ～ ed など。

   We **went swimming** in the sea every day during our holiday in Hawaii.

   On New Year's Day morning, the yard **lay covered** with snow.

4. S＋V＋O＋C（分詞） see＋O＋～ ing/ed, hear＋O＋～ ing/ed, keep＋O＋～ ing/ed など。

   I **heard** someone **singing** my favorite song.

   While I'm absent from school, **keep** me **posted** on our classes.

5. 分詞構文 現在分詞を含む句（～ ing …）が文全体を修飾し、様々な意味を表す。

   ① 時 **Walking** around the mall, I found a new restaurant.

   ＝ While I was walking around the mall, I found a new restaurant.

   Having finished all her chores, she took a shower. （完了形の分詞構文）

   ＝ After she finished all her chores, she took a shower.

   ② 理由 (**Being**) **laid** off, I have to find a job. （受動態の分詞構文）

   ＝ Because I was laid off, I have to find a job.

   ③ 条件 Just **resting** in bed, you'll get over your cold.

   ＝ If you just rest in bed, you'll get over your cold.

   ④ 結果 Camellia oil has the ability to penetrate the deepest layers of the skin, **keeping** it soft and smooth.

   ＝ Camellia oil has the ability to penetrate the deepest layers of the skin and to keep it soft and smooth.

   ⑤ 付帯状況 Sally and I had a good time **talking** over a cup of coffee.

   ＝ Sally and I talked over a cup of coffee and had a good time.

Exercise 9-2: Grammar Exercise

かっこの中の動詞を本文に適合する分詞に変えて、空欄に書き入れなさい。

1. At this time of year, the pavement is always covered with _____ leaves. (fall)

2. A _____ man will catch at a straw. (drown)

3. I saw Melena _____ lunch at the new open-air cafeteria on campus. (eat)

4. I heard my name _____ in the bus. (call)

5. Jerry had his wallet _____ in the crowded train. (steal)

6. Policeman happened to spot a man _____ a woman's bag. (steal)

7. Our club has something special _____ for this three-day weekend. (plan)

Exercise 9-3: Vocabulary Build-up

左の単語と最も近い意味を持つものを右の単語から選びなさい。

1. produced   (A) lasting
2. continuing   (B) manufactured
3. achieving   (C) marketed
4. retaining   (D) supplying
5. expanded   (E) keeping
6. revitalized   (F) extended
7. launched   (G) revived
8. creating   (H) accomplishing
9. included   (I) making
10. giving   (J) contained

CHAPTER 10
Rice

金色の風

No other crop may be as essential in feeding the world as rice. Half the global population depends upon rice as a major source of nutrition. In Asia, rice provides roughly 70 percent of daily calories for more than 2 billion people.

This makes the need to find ways to increase rice productivity especially urgent. While rice on the most productive farms has reached maximum yields, much fertile farmland has been gobbled up for urban expansion. In some places, global warming is increasing night-time temperatures and raising sea levels, further reducing rice production. Although floods, droughts, and storms are expected to increase in the future—again, the result of climate change—fresh water is becoming scarcer. Moreover, certain weeds and pests have become resistant to

herbicides and pesticides. And finally, because the world's population is expected to continue to grow over the next twenty years, experts estimate
15 that rice production will need to increase by at least 30 percent from current levels.

In the 1960s, the first "Green Revolution" enhanced global rice production considerably. Chemical fertilizers and synthetic herbicides and pesticides greatly boosted yields. In addition, the crossbreeding of
20 different kinds of rice led to hardier varieties, bigger harvests, and lower rice prices. These improvements meant that more rice could be grown on less land. From 1961 to 2008, as the human population doubled, food production increased by 150 percent. At the same time, however, only 10 percent of forests and other natural areas was converted to farmland.

25 In 2004, the decoding of the rice genome ushered in the second "Green Revolution." The International Rice Genome Sequencing Project (IRGSP), which was kicked off in 1998, was led by Japanese scientists and ultimately included scientists from 10 nations. Its goal was also to increase rice yields. Rice is the first crop whose genome was decoded and
30 stored in computer data banks around the world.

The decoding of the rice genome should speed up conventional crossbreeding programs. The process of developing a new and better variety of rice and then passing the technology on to farmers is expected to take only three years. In fact, a new strain of rice was already developed
35 in Iwate Prefecture in 2016. The new rice, dubbed "Konjiki-no-kaze" (Wind of Gold), has found great favor among consumers. The rice has a stickier texture and a mildly fragrant flavor. Some say "Konjiki-no-kaze" is one of Japan's best strains.

Notes

63 | *Rice*「米」
1 **No other crop may be as essential in feeding the world as rice.**「世界中の人々を養うのに、米ほど必要不可欠な農作物は他にないかもしれない。」
7 **has been gobbled up for urban expansion**「都市の拡張に飲み込まれてきている」
8 **global warming**「地球温暖化」二酸化炭素などの温室効果ガスの増加によって、地表や海面の温度が上昇する気候変動。
10 **floods, droughts, and storms**「洪水、かんばつ、そして嵐」
11 **fresh water**「真水」

12 **pests**「害虫」

64　13 **herbicides and pesticides**「除草剤や殺虫剤」

16 **current levels**「現在のレベル」

17 **the first "Green Revolution"**「第1次「緑の革命」」1960年代における、高収量品種の開発、化学肥料の使用による農業収穫量の飛躍的増大。

18 **Chemical fertilizers**「化学肥料」

synthetic herbicides and pesticides「合成除草剤及び殺虫剤」

19 **the crossbreeding of different kinds of rice**「様々な種類の米の異種交配」米の品種改良等のために、遺伝子の異なる米の受粉、受精を人為的に行うこと。

20 **hardier varieties**「より丈夫な品種」

21 **rice prices**「米価」

24 **was converted to farmland**「農地に転換された」

25 **the decoding of the rice genome**「米のゲノム解読」ゲノムは、生存に最低限必要な遺伝子を含む染色体のセット。

26 **The International Rice Genome Sequencing Project (IRGSP)**「国際イネゲノム塩基配列プロジェクト（IRGSP）」1998（平成10）年、農林水産省のプロジェクトとして開始され、米国、インド、台湾などが参加。

29 **rice yields**「米の収穫量」

whose genome was decoded and stored in computer data banks around the world「そのゲノムが解読され、世界中のコンピューターのデータバンクに保存された」

33 **passing the technology on to farmers**「その技術を農家に行き渡らせる」

34 **strain**「品種」

35 **Iwate Prefecture**「岩手県」2018（平成30）年、第12回フェミナリーズ世界ワインコンクール（パリ大会）において岩手県花巻市のエーデルワイン（HP http://www.edelwein.co.jp/）の「ドメーヌ・エーデルツヴァイゲルトレーベ 2015 天神ヶ丘畑」が金賞を受賞した。

"Konjiki-no-kaze" (Wind of Gold)「『金色の風』」2016（平成28）年、岩手県がゲノム解析技術を使い開発した米の新品種。「金色」は岩手の黄金文化や稲穂をイメージさせ、「風」は岩手の風土を連想させることから名付けられた。ふわりとした軽やかな食感がありながら、もっちりした粘りがあり、豊かな甘みが口の中に広がるので米としての評価が非常に高い。

36 **has found great favor among consumers**「消費者にとても気に入られた」

The rice has a stickier texture and a mildly fragrant flavor.「この米はより粘り気のある食感があり、そして軽やかなかぐわしい風味をしている。」

37 **Some say "Konjiki-no-kaze" is one of Japan's best strains.**「『金色の風』は日本で最も素晴らしい品種の1つであると言う人もいる。」

Exercise 10-1: COMPREHENSION QUESTIONS

1. Why is rice an essential food crop?
   (A) It is the most versatile of all food crops.
   (B) It is a basic source of nutrition for half the world's people.
   (C) It is easy to grow rice under nearly all conditions.
   (D) Rice is a symbol of traditional culture around the globe.

2. All of the factors below make it important to increase rice production EXCEPT...
   (A) Population decreases
   (B) Loss of farmland to urban areas
   (C) Changes in sea levels
   (D) Plant resistance to herbicides

3. What characterized the first "Green Revolution"?
   (A) Increased demand for rice worldwide
   (B) Scientific breeding programs for making new rice varieties
   (C) Diseases that devastated rice crops
   (D) Use of chemical fertilizers, herbicides, and pesticides

4. What marked the second "Green Revolution"?
   (A) The discovery of plants resistant to all herbicides
   (B) The sequencing of the rice genome
   (C) The collection and centralization of rice data
   (D) The production of rice in urban areas

5. Which of the following is a great benefit resulting from rice genome sequencing?
   (A) Crossbreeding can be done in laboratories.
   (B) Crossbreeding is no longer necessary.
   (C) Creating a better variety takes less time.
   (D) Farmers are no longer confused by advanced technologies.

Grammar Review

Gerund
（動名詞）

動名詞

〈動詞の原形＋ing〉の形を取る動名詞は、「～すること」を意味し、名詞として、主語、補語、目的語などになる。
また動詞としての性質も残し、補語、目的語などを取る。

動名詞の働き

1. 主語として

   Global **warming** is increasing night-time temperatures.

2. 補語として

   My favorite pastime is **playing** video games.

3. 目的語として

   Yuka likes **working** in teams.

4. 前置詞の目的語として

   No other crop may be as essential in **feeding** the world as rice.

5. 動名詞の否定形

   You may regret **not being** nice to your neighbors.

6. 動名詞の受動態

   Mozart didn't like **being called** a genius.

7. 動名詞の完了形

   Terry denied **having been** in a casino all night.

8. 動名詞の主語　所有格で表す

   My wife insisted on **my going** shopping with her.

目的語としての動名詞と不定詞

1. 動名詞だけを目的語にする動詞　admit, consider, enjoy, finish, mind など。

   I'm **considering going** on to graduate school.

2. 不定詞だけを目的語にする動詞　decide, expect, hope, plan, promise, want など。

   Hiroshi **decided to take** part in volunteer work.

3. 動名詞と不定詞の両方を目的語にする動詞　begin, intend, like, start など。

   Unfortunately, it **started raining/to rain**.

4. 目的語が動名詞と不定詞で意味が異なる動詞　forget, regret, remember, try, stop など。

   I clearly **remember locking** the safe.

   Remember to put out the fire in the fireplace.

   I **tried shopping** at a new supermarket.

   I **tried to get** up at five to catch an early train.

Exercise 10-2: Grammar Exercise

次の各文のかっこの中から最も適切な語を選びなさい。

1. We met by chance at the station and stopped (talking / to talk).

2. It may rain tomorrow. Don't forget (bringing / to bring) your umbrella with you.

3. You should avoid (living / to live) in such a dangerous place.

4. I am planning (traveling / to travel) around Europe with my family.

5. It is no use (crying / to cry) over spilt milk.

6. The old house is worth (purchasing / to purchase), if you can afford it.

7. After I graduated from university in Japan, I decided (studying / to study) abroad.

Exercise 10-3: Structure and Idiomatic Expression

次の各文の空欄に最もふさわしい語群をボックスの中から選びなさい。

1. It goes (   ) that the actress is very beautiful.

2. The storm prevented us (   ) out.

3. This book is (   ).

4. I didn't feel (   ) all day yesterday.

5. I was tired of (   ) like a pet.

6. She will never admit (   ) such a thing.

7. I'm looking forward (   ) you in Boston.

(A) like eating   (B) being treated   (C) without saying   (D) from going
(E) to seeing   (F) worth buying   (G) having said

CHAPTER 11
Stress Check

Work-related mental disorders are on the rise. According to the Ministry of Health, Labor and Welfare (MHLW), the number of claims for compensation for poor mental health has been increasing. In the four years between 2010 and 2014, claims grew by over 20 percent, setting a new record. In addition, a 2013 government survey of over 9,000 businesses found that 10 percent of their employees had taken a month's leave or had quit work for mental-health reasons. And although the national suicide rate has been falling for several years, in 2013, the number of suicides related to the workplace increased.

In 2015, a new law went into effect whose aim was to minimize mental-health problems and improve the working environment. All businesses with 50 or more employees were required to make an annual "stress check" available for their employees. This requirement applies to about 18,000 businesses and more than 20 million employees.

15   The stress check is a questionnaire that measures three components of mental health: the causes of stress at work; the symptoms of stress that an employee may be experiencing; and the quality of an employee's personal relationships. Although the Health Ministry version is available to all employers, companies may also opt to create their own questionnaire or
20 to use a standard software program that measures stress. The employer's responsibility is to facilitate the stress check, making it accessible and encouraging employees to take part.

    Although employers must provide the stress check, employees are not required to take it: participation is completely voluntary and confidential.
25 The results are evaluated by mental-health professionals—overseen by doctors and nurses—who share the information directly with each employee. Any employee whose results show him or her to be working under heavy stress may request a doctor's diagnosis. After the diagnosis, the doctor, the employer, and the employee work together to implement
30 any changes needed to remedy the situation.

    Employers do receive aggregated data from the questionnaires, however. The data can help them review existing wellness and employee-assistance programs and policies. The results can also alert employers to possible problems and enable them to make changes—reducing work
35 hours, for example, or arranging personnel transfers—to improve a situation and the overall working environment.

    Some companies have already been making such changes by limiting overtime, designating "no overtime days," and allowing workers to go home early to care for family members.

Notes

69   *Stress Check*「ストレスチェック」勤労者に自己のストレスの程度、原因の把握を促し、職場環境の改善につなげ、勤労者の精神疾患を防ぐためのアンケート式検査。
    1 **mental disorders**「精神的不調」
    are on the rise「増加している」
    the Ministry of Health, Labor and Welfare (MHLW)「厚生労働省（厚労省）」2001（平成13）年発足。

2 **claims**「訴え」

3 **poor mental health**「メンタルヘルスの不調」

6 **leave**「休暇」

7 **the national suicide rate**「全国の自殺率」

10 **a new law**「新法」改正労働安全衛生法（2015〈平成27年〉12月1日施行）。

　went into effect「施行された」

　to minimize「最低限に抑えること」

11 **the working environment**「労働環境」2018（平成30）年6月、働き方改革関連法が成立。時間外労働（残業）に初の罰則付き上限規制を導入し、正規と非正規の労働者の待遇格差を改善する「同一労働同一賃金」など、労働者を保護する施策を多く盛り込んだ。残業上限規制は大企業が2019年4月、中小企業が2020年4月から実施。また高収入の一部専門職を労働時間規制の対象から外す「高度プロフェッショナル制度（高プロ）」を創設した。適用対象を年収1075万円以上の研究職やコンサルタントに限り、高プロ適用後でも労働者本人の意向で撤回できるようにした。

12 **50 or more employees**「50人以上の従業員」

　were required to「～するように求められた」

13 **available**「利用できる」

　This requirement「この要件」

15 **a questionnaire**「アンケート」

　components「構成要件」

16 **the symptoms**「兆候」

17 **personal relationships**「人間関係」

18 **the Health Ministry version**「厚労省版」厚労省作成のアンケート。

20 **a standard software program**「標準ソフトプログラム」

21 **to facilitate**「促進すること」

　making it accessible and encouraging employees to take part「それを利用し易くしたり、従業員に参加を奨励したりして」

23 **must provide**「実施しなければならない」

25 **are evaluated**「評価される」

　overseen「管理される」

28 **a doctor's diagnosis**「医師の診断」

29 **to implement**「実現するために」

31 **aggregated data**「集計データ」

32 **existing wellness and employee-assistance programs and policies**「既存の健康及び従業員支援のプログラムと方策」

34 **reducing work hours, say, or arranging personnel transfers**「例えば労働時間の短縮あるいは人事異動の調整」

37 **by limiting overtime**「残業を制限することで」

38 **designating**「指定して」

　"no overtime days"「「ノー残業ディ」」残業をせず、定時で退社するよう奨励する曜日。

39 **to care for family members**「家族と一緒に過ごすために」

Exercise 11-1: COMPREHENSION QUESTIONS

1. Which of the following is NOT cited as evidence that work-related stress is rising?
   (A) Claims for compensation for poor mental health are increasing.
   (B) A 2013 government survey confirmed the trend.
   (C) Private health and medical data is now being given to employers.
   (D) The number of suicides related to work is increasing.

2. What exactly is the annual stress check?
   (A) It is part of an employee's annual physical examination.
   (B) It measures an employee's productivity.
   (C) It is a survey that all employers must respond to.
   (D) It is an employee questionnaire designed to measure mental stress.

3. How private are the results?
   (A) The results are shared only with the employee.
   (B) The results are passed on to the employer.
   (C) The information about a company's employees is shared with his/her family.
   (D) The central government stores the individual's test results in a public record.

4. All of the following are included in the stress check EXCEPT...
   (A) The quality of an employee's personal relationships
   (B) The symptoms of stress an employee may be showing or undergoing
   (C) Physical data such as blood pressure and pulse rate
   (D) The causes of an employee's possible work-related stress

5. What can employers do to create a better work environment?
   (A) Comply with all national and local laws
   (B) Review and improve existing employee well-being and working-hour policies
   (C) Encourage employees to work longer hours
   (D) Suggest that employees with excessive stress change companies

Grammar Review

Infinitive
（不定詞）

不定詞
〈to＋動詞の原形〉と、動詞の原形だけの原形不定詞がある。

不定詞の用法

1. 名詞用法「～すること」
① 主語として　**To have** good meals is essential to your health.
② 形式主語 it が不定詞を受ける　**It**'s next to impossible **to beat** him at chess.
③ 補語として　The new law's aim was **to minimize** mental-health problems and **improve** the working environment.
④ 目的語として　Dad promised **to take** me to a ball game.
⑤ 形式目的語 it が不定詞を受ける　I found **it** hard **to keep** the secret.

2. 形容詞用法　不定詞が前の名詞を修飾する。「～する…」「～するための…」
① 名詞が不定詞の主語　They were the first **couple to come** to the dance.
② 名詞が不定詞の目的語　I have some **homework to do** this evening.
③ 不定詞が名詞を説明する　We had no **chance to talk** to the senator.

3. 副詞用法　不定詞が動詞、形容詞、副詞、文全体を修飾し、様々な意味を表す。
① 目的「～するために」Kate cuts down on sugar **to stay** slim.
② 原因「～して」I'm absolutely delighted **to work** with you.
③ 理由「～するとは」I was a fool **to believe** a story like that.
④ 結果「結局～した」He tried to carry out his unworkable plan, only **to give** it up.
⑤ 形容詞＋不定詞「～するのに…」This computer is **easy to use**.
⑥ 独立用法　**To put it in a nutshell**, I want you to work a little harder.

4. 目的格補語としての不定詞
① 動詞（allow, enable, expect, get, want など）＋目的語＋不定詞

　　The results can **enable them to make** changes to improve a situation.
② 使役動詞（make, have, let）＋目的語＋原形不定詞

　　What **makes you think** so?

　　We **had Tom mow** our lawn.

　　Please **let me know** if there's something I can do.
③ 知覚動詞（see, hear, feel など）＋目的語＋原形不定詞

　　I **saw them shake** hands.

　　I **heard someone call** my name.

　　I **felt someone pat** me on the shoulder.

Exercise 11-2: Grammar Exercise

かっこ内の語句を並び替えて、日本文に合う英文を作りなさい。

1. 私は英語の辞書なしでもこの小説を読むのが易しいと分かった。
   (an English dictionary / easy / found / I / it / novel / read / to / this / without)

2. 私は風邪を予防するためにいつも帰宅するとすぐにうがいをする。
   (colds / always / as / as / prevent / gargle / get / home / I / I / soon / to)

3. 温かい飲み物をいただけませんか？
   (drink / I / may / have / hot / something / to / ?)

4. 私の友達たちは私たちの結婚を祝うために盛大なパーティーをしてくれた。
   (a / big / celebrate / gave / marriage / my friends / our / party / to / us)

5. 彼は大人になり、全世界で大きな影響を与える思想家になった。
   (all / around / a thinker / be / great / grew / had / he / influence / to / the world / up / who)

Exercise 11-3: Vocabulary Build-up

左の単語と最も反対に近い意味を持つものを右の単語から選びなさい。

1. mental   (A) amateur
2. employee   (B) employer
3. minimize   (C) exception
4. health   (D) illness
5. improve   (E) maximize
6. reduce   (F) partly
7. standard   (G) physical
8. completely   (H) increase
9. result   (I) cause
10. professional   (J) worsen

CHAPTER 12
Generic Drugs

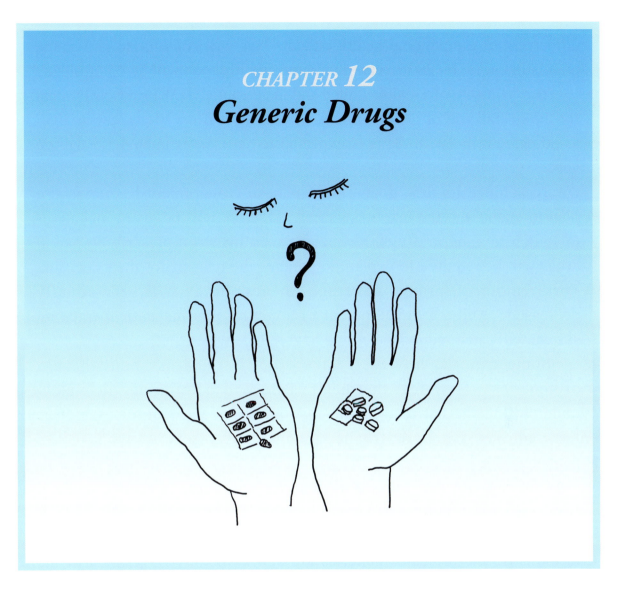

Generic drugs are cheaper versions of brand-name drugs whose patent protection has expired. Although they are identical to new drugs in dosage, quality, strength, and safety, generic drugs are typically sold at a reduced price.

Brand-name drugs are more expensive because pharmaceutical companies develop them under patent protection. The patent protects the company's sole right to sell a drug at a price that covers the company's costs for initial research and development (R&D). But once these patents expire, other manufacturers are free to sell generics more cheaply.

Generics offer both consumers and hospitals considerable savings. For this reason, the Japanese Government is promoting the increased use of generics to help cut rising prescription costs, which represent roughly

20 percent of the national health budget. This will continue to rise as the population ages: by 2035, one in three people in Japan will be 65 or older.

15 The Ministry of Health, Labor and Welfare (MHLW) revised its goal for the overall use of generic drugs, increasing it from 70 percent in 2017 to 80 percent in 2020. This is expected to save an estimated 1.5 trillion yen.

To achieve its new goals, the Japanese Government has devised a
20 plan to encourage the use of generics. Doctors will be given incentives to switch to generic drugs. Physicians who insist on prescribing patent drugs will be required to explain to patients the reasons for their decision. Furthermore, insurance coverage for new drugs will be gradually decreased. And the development of a central pharmaceutical tracking
25 system will catch redundancies and help reduce waste.

Some experts, however, have voiced concerns about the use of generics. They fear that health care will deteriorate, ultimately undercutting the national health-insurance system. More research is required, they say, to determine how effectively generics work in real
30 patients.

Others doubt that the use of generics will actually reduce medical costs. Generics are more expensive in Japan than in other countries, their prices being about 60 percent of those of patented drugs. In comparison, in the U.S., the prices of generics are approximately 20 percent of the
35 patented counterparts.

Another challenge facing the government plan is to gain the trust of patients. Most patients in Japan prefer brand-name drugs, believing that generic equivalents are somehow inferior. This preference, reinforced by pharmaceutical companies' ad campaigns, must be countered with accurate
40 information about generics.

Notes

75 *Generic Drugs* = generics 「ジェネリック医薬品」後発医薬品。新薬の特許が切れた後に販売される同じ成分の薬。新薬と同じ効果をより安い価格で提供する。
　1 **cheaper versions** 「廉価版」より安価な製品。
　　brand-name drugs whose patent protection has expired 「特許権の保護が期限切れになったブランド薬」

2 **patent protection**「特許権の保護」2018（平成 30）年 5 月、インターネット上での著作物の利用を拡大する改正著作権法が成立。著作権者の許諾を得なくても書籍などを電子データ化でき、書籍の検索や論文などに盗用がないかを検証しやすくする。ネット活用が進む教育現場でも新聞などを教材として使いやすくする規制緩和を盛り込んだ。2019(平成 31)年 1 月 1 日施行。

3 **dosage**「用量」
strength「効能」
at a reduced price「低価格で」

5 **pharmaceutical companies**「製薬会社」

6 **under patent protection**「特許権の保護の下に」

7 **sole right**「独占権」

8 **research and development (R&D)**「研究開発（R&D）」

10 **offer**「もたらす」

12 **prescription costs**「薬剤費」
represent「に当たる」

13 **the national health budget**「国の医療予算」
as the population ages「人口が高齢化するにつれて」

14 **65 or older**「65 歳以上」

15 **The Ministry of Health, Labor and Welfare (MHLW)**「厚生労働省（厚労省）」2001（平成 13）年発足。

19 **has devised a plan**「計画をまとめた」

20 **will be given incentives to switch to generic drugs**「ジェネリック医薬品に変えるための優遇措置を与えられるだろう」

21 **prescribing patent drugs**「特許薬を処方すること」

23 **insurance coverage**「保険補填額」国民健康保険等で補われる金額。

24 **a central pharmaceutical tracking system**「医薬品の中央追跡システム」医薬品の流れを一括して把握するシステム。

25 **redundancies**「余剰薬」

26 **have voiced concerns**「懸念の声を上げてきた」

27 **health care**「ヘルスケア：医療」
deteriorate「〜の質が低下する」

28 **undercutting**「損なう」
the national health-insurance system「国民健康保険システム」

29 **to determine how effectively generics work in real patients**「ジェネリック医薬品が実際の患者にどの位効果的に作用するかを決めるために」

33 **In comparison**「それに比べ」

34 **the patented counterparts**「相当する特許薬」

36 **challenge**「課題」

38 **generic equivalents**「ジェネリック医薬品の同等品」

39 **must be countered**「反証されなければならない」

Exercise 12-1: COMPREHENSION QUESTIONS

1. What precisely is a generic drug?
   (A) An inferior version of a brand-name drug
   (B) A brand-name drug still under patent protection
   (C) A new drug developed to replace an older drug
   (D) An equivalent of a brand-name drug that is no longer under patent protection

2. Which of the following best describes the protection that a patent gives a pharmaceutical company?
   (A) It ensures that the company that develops and tests a drug is the only one to sell it.
   (B) It guarantees that new drugs will be developed.
   (C) It prevents consumers from buying generics.
   (D) It guarantees that the drug is safe and effective.

3. What is the trend for prescription costs in Japan as the population ages?
   (A) They are likely to go down over the next few years.
   (B) They cannot be predicted.
   (C) They are likely to rise significantly.
   (D) They will stay about the same.

4. Which of these is the best description of the Government's position on generics?
   (A) The Government disapproves of them.
   (B) The Government has no plan for them.
   (C) The Government supports their increased use.
   (D) The Government continues to recommend patent drugs.

5. Which of the following is NOT a challenge facing the increased use of generic drugs?
   (A) Increasing the prices of generic drugs even further
   (B) Finding more experts to approve generics
   (C) Gaining the public's trust
   (D) Collecting accurate information about generics

Grammar Review

Preposition
（前置詞）

前置詞
前置詞は、名詞、代名詞、動名詞などの前に置かれ、形容詞句または副詞句を作る。

様々な前置詞

1. 場所、方向を表す前置詞
① at「～で / の」（地点）　in「～で / の」（範囲）
　　I got my prescription **at** the pharmacy.
　　Most patients **in** Japan prefer brand-name drugs.
② above「～の上に / の」　below「～の下に / の」（位置、程度）
　　the moon just **above** the horizon　ten degrees **below** zero
③ over「～の上に / の」　under「～の下に / の」（位置、程度、関係）
　　bridges **over** a river　new drugs **under** patent protection
④ on「～の上に / の」（接触）
　　I see a huge spider **on** the ceiling!

2. 時を表す前置詞
① at「～に」（時刻）　on「～に」（日）　in「～に」（午前 / 午後、週、月、年など）
　　at five o'clock on the dot　**on** Christmas Day　late **in** the afternoon　**in** fall, 2015
② within「～以内に」　in「～後に」　after「～より後に」
　　within a week　**in** a few days　**after** January 3
③ till/until「～まで」　by「～までに」
　　Kyoto was Japan's capital **till/until** the mid-19th century.
　　I have to hand in my history essay **by** Friday.
④ for「～の間」（ある時間の間）　during「～の間」（ある行事などの間）
　　I haven't seen my high school classmates **for** 20 years.
　　We'll have a lot of foreign visitors **during** the Olympics.

3. その他の前置詞
① by「～で」（手段）　with「～で」（道具）
　　We're going to travel all around South America **by** bicycle.
　　Takeshi fixed my bag's zipper **with** a pair of pliers.
② in「～で」（状態）　into「～に」（状態の変化）
　　I get some exercise every day, and I'm **in** great shape.
　　She talked her husband **into** quitting smoking.
③ 前置詞句　across from「～の向かいに」、because of「～のために」、for the purpose of「～の目的で」、
　　in front of「～の前で」、in spite of「～にもかかわらず」など。
　　I have to decline your offer **because of** my poor health.
　　In spite of being such a large city, Tokyo has a lot of greenery.

Exercise 12-2: Grammar Exercise

( )の中に適する前置詞を入れなさい。

1. I got home late and then I had dinner (   ) midnight.

2. I must finish this work (   ) noon.

3. The express train (   ) Kyoto left just one minute ago.

4. The little boy accidentally jumped out (   ) the window.

5. As (   ) me, I hope to visit the museum again very soon.

6. He does things his own way, but he looks up (   ) his parents.

7. He takes (   ) his father in looks and his mother in temperament.

8. I called (   ) my friend at his house and we walked to school together.

9. Have you heard (   ) your friend who went to England?

10. He is proud (   ) his high school's victory at Koshien Stadium.

Exercise 12-3: Listening Practice

CD を聞いて空欄に正しい語を入れなさい。

The Ministry of Health, Labor and Welfare (MHLW) revised its goal for the overall use of generic drugs, increasing it (1.   ) 70 percent in 2017 to 80 percent (2.   ) 2020. This is expected to save an estimated 1.5 trillion yen.

To achieve its new goals, the Japanese Government has devised a plan to encourage the use of generics. Doctors will be given incentives to switch to generic drugs, with physicians who insist (3.   ) prescribing patent drugs being required to explain (4.   ) patients the reasons for their decision. Furthermore, insurance coverage for new drugs will be gradually decreased. And the development (5.   ) a central pharmaceutical tracking system will catch redundancies and help reduce waste.

CHAPTER 13
Self-driving Cars

The next wave of automotive evolution has arrived with the introduction of self-driving cars, also called autonomous or driverless cars. As the vehicles go into wider use, experts predict a smoother flow of traffic and greater safety. Nearly all traffic accidents—90 percent—are caused by operator errors. Unlike human drivers, self-driving cars cannot be distracted, fall asleep, or fail to react quickly to changing traffic conditions. Self-driving cars turn the steering wheel, apply the brakes, and press the accelerator automatically using information about environmental conditions gathered from sensors, cameras, and satellites.

There are four levels of automation. At the first level, the system controls just one of the three most important functions: steering, braking, or acceleration. With the second level, the system controls at least two of those functions. In third-level vehicles, the system controls all three basic functions, but a human driver can intervene if necessary. Fourth-level cars 15 are fully automatic. No human is involved in operating the car, leaving drivers free to watch TV, read, or chat on their phones, for example, while riding in their cars.

The advent of increasingly automated vehicles is raising many practical challenges. One is how to program driverless cars to obey 20 traffic laws—speed limits, traffic lights, and so on. Another hurdle is deciding who is liable when a self-driving car causes an accident, injures someone, or damages property. The owner of the car? The manufacturer? Additionally, financial investment will be needed to carry out changes to the infrastructure. Older, narrow roads may have to be widened. New 25 sidewalks to protect pedestrians and bike lanes that keep bicycles separate from automotive traffic will have to be built.

Another thorny issue is the interface between the automated vehicle and the owner-driver. When the system, sometimes called a "robo-chauffeur," needs assistance, there has to be a way to communicate with 30 the human driver-owner. Visual warnings alone are usually not enough to alert a driver. Therefore, some manufacturers have added a combination of sensors and alarms: lights, spoken instructions, or even physical stimulation such as vibrating seats. Despite these concerns, given the public's enthusiasm for these new cars, sales are likely to boom.

Notes

81   *Self-driving Cars* = autonomous cars, driverless cars 「自動運転車」IT を駆使し運転者がハンドルやブレーキ操作をしなくても走行する車。渋滞の解消や事故の減少が期待されている。

1 **has arrived with the introduction of**「〜の導入と共に到来した」

3 **go into wider use**「より広く実用化される」

5 **operator errors**「運転者のミス」

6 **fail to react quickly to changing traffic conditions**「変化する交通状況に素早く対応し損なう」

7 **Self-driving cars turn the steering wheel, apply the brakes, and press the accelerator automatically using information about environmental conditions gathered from sensors, cameras, and satellites.**「センサー、カメラ、そして衛星から集められた環境の条件についての情報を使用して、自動運転車は自動的にハンドルを回し、ブレーキを掛け、そしてアクセルを踏む。」2018（平成 30）年 4 月に実際の測位システムの運用が始まった準天頂衛星「みちびき」は常に日本の上空にあるので、車の位置情報の誤差が数センチまで縮まるとされ、日本政府が目指す自動運転車の普及に貢献しそうである。

10 **There are four levels of automation.**「自動化には 4 つのレベルがある。」現在これをベースにし

て、自動運転にはレベル0〜5の段階がある。レベル0：ドライバーがすべてを操作。レベル1：システムがハンドル操作、あるいはアクセル、ブレーキのどれか1つをサポート。レベル2：システムがハンドル操作やアクセル、ブレーキのどれか2つをサポート。レベル3：特定の場所でシステムが全てを操作し、緊急時はドライバーが操作。レベル4：高速道路のような特定の場所でシステムが全てを操作。レベル5：場所の特定なくシステムが全てを操作。レベル3〜5が自動運転で、特にレベル5は完全自動運転。

11 **controls just one**「1つだけを制御する」
  steering, braking, or acceleration「ハンドル、ブレーキ、あるいはアクセル（加速）」

82 14 **intervene**「介入する」
  if necessary「もし必要があれば」

15 **No human is involved in operating the car, leaving drivers free to watch TV, read, or chat on their phones,**「人間は車の運転に関与せず、ドライバーには、自由にテレビを見たり、本を読んだり、あるいは電話で話したりさせる」

18 **The advent**「登場」
  is raising many practical challenges「多くの実際的課題を引き起こしている」

19 **how to program**「どのようにプログラムするか」

20 **traffic laws**「交通法規」

21 **who is liable**「誰に責任があるか」

22 **damages property**「器物を破損したり」

23 **financial investment**「金融投資」
  changes「作り替え」

24 **the infrastructure**「インフラ」インフラストラクチャー。エネルギー、交通、通信などの社会経済基盤。

25 **bike lanes**「自転車レーン」

27 **thorny issue**「厄介な問題」
  interface「インターフェイス」接点。

28 **a "robo-chauffeur,"**「「ロボット運転手」」

30 **Visual warnings alone**「目で見る警告だけでは」
  to alert「知らせるのに」

32 **spoken instructions**「音声指示」
  physical stimulation「体への刺激」

33 **given the public's enthusiasm for these new cars**「これらの新しい車への一般の人々の熱い支持があれば」

Exercise 13-1: COMPREHENSION QUESTIONS

1. What are the major benefits of autonomous cars?
   - (A) They are much cheaper to buy and operate.
   - (B) They are fuel efficient.
   - (C) They will reduce traffic congestion and accidents.
   - (D) Their futuristic designs appeal to young drivers.

2. All of these technologies support self-driving cars EXCEPT...
   - (A) sensors that gauge traffic
   - (B) satellites to monitor the car's movement
   - (C) cameras
   - (D) more comfortable interiors

3. Which of the following describes third-level cars?
   - (A) Full automation
   - (B) Automation of steering and braking
   - (C) Automation of acceleration and braking
   - (D) Automation of all three basic driving functions

4. What is one important issue that must be solved?
   - (A) Liability for accidents
   - (B) Eligibility to buy the cars
   - (C) Marketing the new technology
   - (D) Increasing the car's longevity

5. How does a robo-chauffeur communicate with a human?
   - (A) It calls out to the human driver.
   - (B) Multiple signals are usually necessary to alert the human driver.
   - (C) It sends a text message to the human driver.
   - (D) It shuts the car off automatically.

Grammar Review

Conjunction
（接続詞）

等位接続詞　単語、語句、文を対等の関係で結び付ける。and, but, for, nor, or, so など。

1.　注意すべき and の用法
① a 〜 and 〜「〜兼〜」Ogai Mori was a doctor **and** writer.
② 命令文 + and …「〜しなさい。そうすれば…」Knock, **and** the door will open.

2.　注意すべき but の用法
① not 〜 but …「〜ではなく…」The fault is **not** yours **but** mine.
② not only 〜 but (also) …「〜だけでなく…」She is **not only** smart **but also** hardworking.

3.　注意すべき or の用法
① not 〜 or 〜「〜も〜も…ない」I don't drink **or** smoke.
② 命令文 + or …「〜しなさい。そうしないと…」Be careful, **or** you'll get in trouble.

従属接続詞
1.　名詞節を導く従属接続詞　whether, that など。名詞節は目的語句などになる。
① whether「〜かどうか」Do you know **whether** Pat will come to the dinner?
② that「〜ということ」I heard **that** there was a big discovery.

2.　副詞節を導く従属接続詞　副詞節は従属節として主節を修飾する。
① 時　after, as, as soon as, before, since, until/till, when, while など。
　　As the vehicles go into wider use, experts predict a smoother flow of traffic and greater safety.
② 原因・理由　as, because, since など。
　　I was late for work **because** my car broke down.
③ 条件　if, once, unless など。
　　If it rains, I'll stay home.
④ 譲歩　although, even if, no matter what/how, though, whether 〜 or not など。
　　You have to eat vegetables **whether** you like them **or not**.
⑤ 様態　as, as if, as though など。
　　The nurse took care of the elderly woman **as if** she was her own mother.
⑥ 制限　as long as, as far as など。
　　Don't let the kids play outside **as long as** they like.

3.　従属接続詞を含む慣用表現
① hardly 〜 when …　「〜するとすぐに…」
　　She had **hardly** hung up the phone **when** another call came in.
② so that 〜 can …「〜が…できるように」
　　Speak up a little **so that** Grandpa **can** hear you.

Exercise 13-2: Grammar Exercise

2-19

次の各文の空欄に最もふさわしい語をボックスの中から選びなさい。

1. You can try reading this novel, (　　　　) don't expect it to be an easy read.

2. Do you want to go out somewhere, (　　　　) stay at home tonight and just relax?

3. I can't go to bed (　　　　) I finish my homework.

4. I worked hard in order (　　　　) I might save enough to buy the latest smartphone.

5. It is seven years (　　　　) the Tohoku region was hit by disaster.

6. I won't be able to open a new business (　　　　) the bank gives me a loan.

7. (　　　　) it was snowy and very cold, Sarah went out without a coat.

(A) but	(B) or	(C) since	(D) that
(E) till	(F) though	(G) unless	

Exercise 13-3: Structure and Idiomatic Expression

2-20

次の各文の空欄に最もふさわしい語群をボックスの中から選びなさい。

1. It looked (　　　　) it were going to cloud over and rain.

2. She passed the exam (　　　　) not having studied for it.

3. (　　　　) he tries to stop me, I will go.

4. Take this credit card with you (　　　　) you need it for an emergency.

5. He walked carefully (　　　　) he would fall.

6. We ought to leave early (　　　　) we not miss the Shinkansen.

7. (　　　　) my ex-girlfriend saw me, she stood up and left.

(A) as if	(B) even if	(C) for fear that	(D) in case
(E) in order that	(F) in spite of	(G) the moment	

CHAPTER *14*
Renewable Energy

Many rural areas in Japan are in decline as more and more young people migrate to large cities, leaving behind an aging population. Older farmers are often unable to maintain the countryside's traditional landscape. The loss of this landscape, noted for its harmonious blend of nature and farmland, is causing serious environmental problems. Poorly-maintained forests absorb less carbon dioxide (CO_2) and cannot retain water. These problems underlie the economic woes that rural regions are now experiencing.

One key to rural revitalization lies in renewable energy. Rural areas are especially blessed in renewable energy sources: solar, wind, and even geothermal power, which is produced by heat from inside the earth. People in villages and small towns are among the most enthusiastic supporters of renewable energy. As many as 100 local renewable energy projects are under way around the country. For example, renewable energy, including solar energy, now provides over 90 percent of the energy requirements in a year in Nagano Prefecture.

According to a 2015 report from the Ministry of Economy, Trade, and Industry (METI), renewable energy use will continue to increase in the years ahead. By 2030, renewable energy will supply between 22 and 24 percent of the nation's energy needs, up from 12 percent in 2015. Nuclear energy use is expected to plummet to 22 percent from the 53 percent predicted in 2010. In addition, liquefied natural gas (LNG) is estimated to provide about 44 percent of energy demand, and coal, 31 percent. Imports of oil will cover any gaps in supply.

Consumers are increasingly adamant in voicing the need to use energy more efficiently. These advocates believe that good energy practices begin with individuals. One movement that is attracting a growing number of fans is living off-grid. Living off-grid refers to living in a self-sufficient way, without relying on power from a public utility company or similar public services, like water and sewage.

Living off-grid requires generating enough energy to meet one's needs, usually through solar packs or wind systems reminiscent of old-fashioned windmills. By designing homes that feature large windows, efficient ventilation, and good insulation, off-grid heating and cooling needs can be significantly reduced.

Cities are taking the lead in advocating renewable energy. In 2015, the mayors and representatives of Japan's 19 largest cities, whose combined population of over 27 million is about one-fifth the country's total, called for a substantial increase in renewables use by 2030. Called "30 by 30," the goal is to boost renewable energy use to 30 percent, exceeding the national goal.

Notes

87　***Renewable Energy*** 「再生可能エネルギー」石油などの化石エネルギーとは異なる、太陽光、風力、地熱、バイオマスなど短期間で再生可能なエネルギー。

1 **rural areas** 「田舎の地域」

2 migrate「移住する」

an aging population「高齢化する人口」

4 its harmonious blend of nature and farmland「その自然と農地の調和の取れた組み合わせ」

5 environmental problems「環境問題」

Poorly-maintained forests「うまく維持されていない森」

6 carbon dioxide (CO_2)「二酸化炭素」

7 underlie the economic woes「経済的困難の根底にある」

9 rural revitalization「地方再活性化」

10 solar「太陽光」

11 geothermal power「地熱発電」

12 are among「～の一つである」

13 renewable energy projects「再生可能エネルギープロジェクト」

are under way「進行中である」

15 the energy requirements「電力必要量」

16 Nagano Prefecture「長野県」長野県では、自然エネルギーをビジネスとして地域に普及させることを通じて、エネルギー、地域資金、人（雇用）の地域内循環により社会経済の活性化を図る「自然エネルギー100％自給型コミュニティづくり」を推進している。

17 the Ministry of Economy, Trade, and Industry (METI)「経済産業省（経産省）」2001（平成13）年、通商産業省（通産省）から改称。

19 will supply「賄うだろう」

20 the nation's energy needs「全国のエネルギー需要」

Nuclear energy use「原子力エネルギーの使用」

21 plummet「急落する」

22 liquefied natural gas (LNG)「液化天然ガス（LNG）」天然ガスを冷却した液体燃料。

24 will cover any gaps in supply「供給の不足を賄うだろう」

25 are increasingly adamant in voicing「益々強固に訴えている」

26 advocates「支持者たち」

good energy practices「エネルギー使用の良い習慣」

28 living off-grid「オフグリッド生活」公共的に提供されるエネルギーに頼らない生活。

in a self-sufficient way「自給自足のやり方で」

29 power「電力」

a public utility company「公益事業会社」

30 water and sewage「水道及び下水道」

31 to meet one's needs「ある人の需要を満たすのに」

32 solar packs「太陽光設備」太陽光発電設備一式。

wind systems「風力システム」風力発電システム。

reminiscent of「～を思い出させる」

34 ventilation「換気」

insulation「断熱」

36 are taking the lead「先頭に立っている」

37 whose combined population of over 27 million is about one-fifth the country's total「その合計2700万人以上の人口が全国総計の約5分の1である」

39 renewables use「再生可能エネルギーの使用」

"30 by 30,"「「30までに30」」再生可能エネルギーの使用を2030年までに30％に増やす目標。

40 exceeding the national goal「国の目標を上回り」

Exercise 14-1: COMPREHENSION QUESTIONS

1. Why do Japan's rural areas need revitalization?
   (A) An aging farming population is leading to environmental problems.
   (B) As the population ages, more people are moving to the countryside.
   (C) Rural communities are reluctant to use renewable energy.
   (D) Farmland is becoming less productive.

2. What is one consequence of poorly-maintained forests mentioned in the reading?
   (A) Inferior wood products
   (B) Loss of Japan's traditional customs
   (C) Damage to nearby farmland
   (D) Reduced absorption of carbon dioxide from the atmosphere

3. What role can rural areas play in increasing renewable energy use?
   (A) They play only a limited role because they lack renewable energy sources.
   (B) They are a potential source of much renewable energy.
   (C) They are reluctant to switch to renewables.
   (D) They are exporting solar and wind power to energy-starved large cities.

4. Which of these best describes living off-grid?
   (A) A primitive lifestyle with few conveniences
   (B) A growing trend in urban areas
   (C) A self-reliant lifestyle
   (D) More efficient use of public utilities

5. What is one goal for renewables use by 2030?
   (A) To supply 53 percent of Japan's energy needs
   (B) To reduce government energy costs
   (C) To increase use of renewables by 30 percent by 2030
   (D) To decrease energy imports to under 20 percent

Grammar Review

Subjunctive Mood
（仮定法）

仮定法
現在の事実に反する仮定を述べる仮定法過去と、過去の事実に反する仮定を述べる仮定法過去完了がある。

仮定法過去

1. 形と意味

〈If＋主語＋動詞の過去形＋…, 主語＋would/could/might/should＋動詞の原形＋….〉
「もしも〜したら、…するだろう。」if節が後置されることもある。if節のbe動詞はwereが正用法だが、口語ではwasが使われることもある。

2. 仮定法過去の用法

① 現在の事実に反する仮定

If I **were**/**was** in your shoes, I **would take** some action right away.

② 実現しそうにない未来の仮定

Your friend **would be** let down if you **didn't keep** your promise.

③ if節の省略

Boosting renewable energy use to 30 percent **would be** great.

仮定法過去完了

1. 形と意味

〈If＋主語＋had＋過去分詞＋…, 主語＋would/could/might/should＋have＋過去分詞＋….〉「もしも〜していたら、…しただろう。」

2. 仮定法過去完了の用法

① 過去の事実に反する仮定

If he **had seen** a doctor earlier, he **could have recovered** more quickly.

② if節の省略

You **should have thought** twice before marrying a man like that.

if節の代わりをする語句

1. with「〜があれば」　I could have gotten a better job **with** a better education.
2. but for, without「〜がなければ」　**But for** one small mistake, I would have scored 100 on the test.
3. otherwise「そうでなければ」　I'm glad we had a map; **otherwise**, we would have gotten lost.

I wish＋仮定法

1. I wish＋主語＋動詞の過去形「〜だったらいいのに。」　**I wish** I **were** talented at music.
2. I wish＋主語＋had＋過去分詞「〜だったらよかったのに。」　**I wish** I **had set** out earlier.

Exercise 14-2: Grammar Exercise

次の各文の空欄に最もふさわしい語群をボックスの中から選びなさい。

1. If my grandfather (　　　) alive, he would have helped me.
2. I won't be able to provide for my family (　　　) I work harder.
3. If I (　　　) a novelist, I would write a novel which makes people happy.
4. If I (　　　) tell her all I know, she would be amazed.
5. He spends money (　　　) he were a billionaire.
6. I wish I (　　　) him play at Wimbledon.
7. If I had a lot of money, I (　　　) more generous.

> (A) as if　(B) could see　(C) had been　(D) unless
> (E) were　(F) were to　(G) would be

Exercise 14-3: Vocabulary Build-up

次の各語の定義として最もふさわしいものを(A)〜(G)の中から選びなさい。

1. migrate
2. geothermal
3. nuclear
4. advocate
5. ventilation
6. predict
7. supply

(A) to publicly support a particular way of doing something
(B) to move to another area or country, especially in order to find work
(C) to say that something will happen, before it happens
(D) the energy produced when the nucleus of an atom is either split or joined with the nucleus of another atom
(E) an amount of something that is available to be used
(F) relating to or coming from the heat inside the earth
(G) the letting in of fresh air into a room, building, etc.

CHAPTER 15
3D Printers

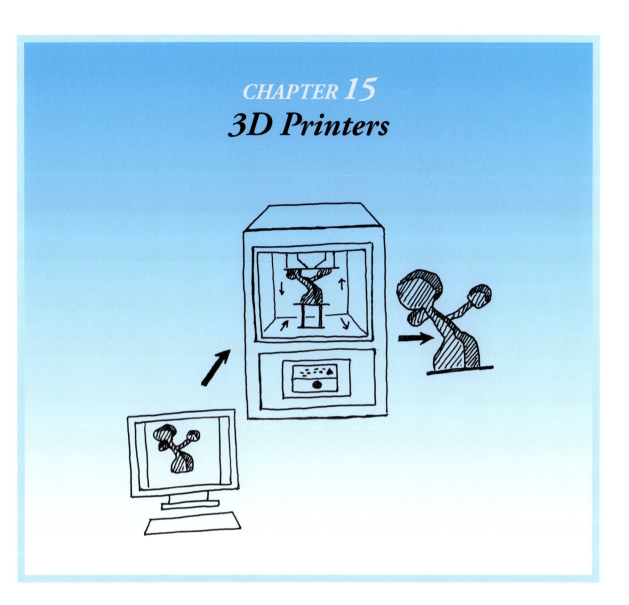

The term "3D printer" refers to a device that forms a variety of objects based on three-dimentional (3-D) digital data. The process is also called additive manufacturing (AM), because the "printed" object is formed by successive applications of layer upon layer of material. Each layer represents a very thin cross-section of the final object. Using the process, objects of nearly any size, shape, color, or material can be synthesized.

The process has two main components. The first step is to create digital computer data that, in essence, tells the printing machine exactly what to do. The item to be replicated has to be divided into thousands of horizontal layers. This step, called "slicing," is done by a computer-program or software installed in a 3D printer. The information is then downloaded to the printer through a USB port or wireless Internet

connection. The second step is the actual printing of the object by applying successive layers of whatever material the printer is loaded with. 3D
15 printers can produce objects from a wide range of materials, including malleable plastics, metals, metal alloys, and ceramics.

Invented in the 1980s, 3D-printer technology is being put to use today in many innovative ways. Several businesses in the heart of Japan's traditional arts and crafts region, for instance, are embracing 3D
20 printers. Unique designs for ceramics, porcelain, and lacquerware can be transformed into real objects more quickly and accurately with a 3D printer than by human workers.

The 3D printer has also changed the field of prosthetics, or the creation of artificial limbs. Previously, artificial limbs were hard to come by and
25 extremely expensive; an artificial arm cost about 1.5 million yen. But using a 3D printer, one Japanese company has built an artificial hand for only 30,000 yen. Although the final price of an artificial limb may rise, it will still likely be much cheaper than traditional prostheses. This is a wonderful development, especially for handicapped children who often are
30 denied a prosthetic device until they are fully grown.

The creation of human tissue by 3D printer is a major challenge for regenerative medicine. The process, called "bioprinting," uses a mixture of human stem cells, water, and a bio-degradable material to give the printed cells structure. Scientists are looking into ways to use the printing process
35 to make skin, blood vessels, and cartilage. The ultimate goal is to produce whole organs.

Notes

93   *3D Printers* = three-dimensional printers「3D プリンター」。3D（3 次元）のデジタルデータをもとに、立体を形づくる装置。積層造形装置、3 次元プリンターともいう。一般的なプリンターが 2 次元で紙に印刷するように、3 次元の物体を一層一層、積層させながら造形するため、このような名称で呼ばれる。3D プリンターにより、立体の製品を短時間かつ低コストで生産できる。
2 **digital data** 「デジタルデータ」コンピューター等で扱われる情報。
  The process 「その製法」
3 **additive manufacturing (AM)** 「積層造形法（AM）」粉末状あるいは液状の樹脂、合金等の材料を一層ずつ積み重ねることにより、製品を造形する方法。
  because the "printed" object is formed by successive applications of layer upon layer of material 「「プリント」される物が材料を幾層にも連続して積層することで造形されるので」

4 **Each layer represents a very thin cross-section of the final object.**「一つひとつの層は完成品の非常に薄い断面を表している。」

8 **tells**「伝える」

the printing machine「プリンター」

9 **The item to be replicated**「複製されることになるアイテム（物）」

10 **"slicing,"**「「スライシング」」コンピューター上で、物品のモデルとなるイメージを薄く輪切りにし、その輪郭に沿うように、材料を噴射するプリンターのヘッドの移動を設定すること。

12 **USB port**「USB ポート」Universal Serial Bus。コンピューター等に機器をつなぐ接続部の規格の１つ。

94 | 13 **the actual printing of the object by applying successive layers of whatever material the printer is loaded with**「プリンターに入力されたあらゆる材料の層を連続して積層することによる実際的な物のプリンティング」

16 **malleable plastics**「可鍛性プラスチック」熱溶解したプラスチック。

metal alloys「合金」銅合金などの粉末。

17 **is being put to use**「実用化されつつある」

18 **the heart of Japan's traditional arts and crafts region**「日本の伝統的美術工芸地域の中心地」

19 **are embracing**「進んで採り入れている」

20 **ceramics**「セラミックス」陶器の材料。

porcelain「磁器」石粉を材料にして焼いた器。

lacquerware「漆器（しっき）」京都金閣寺や岩手県平泉の金色堂、日光東照宮、そして皇居正門の修理修復に岩手県浄法寺産の漆が使用されている。岩手県・（株）浄法寺漆産業はこの漆や漆器の販路を積極的に国内外に広げている。（株）浄法寺漆産業 HP http://www.japanjoboji.com

23 **prosthetics, or the creation of artificial limbs**「人工器官技術あるいは人工義肢の製作」病気、事故等で失われた手足の形態、機能を復元する人工義肢の作成。

25 **an artificial arm**「義腕」

26 **an artificial hand**「義手」

30 **a prosthetic device**「人工補助用具」

31 **human tissue**「人体の組織」

challenge「課題」

32 **regenerative medicine**「再生医療」臓器等の組織が失われた、あるいは機能しなくなった場合に、移植等によって失われた機能を回復する医療。

"bioprinting,"「「バイオプリンティング」」3D プリンターを用いて細胞組織を作成する医療技術。

33 **stem cells**「幹細胞」分裂等によって新たな細胞を生み出す能力を持つ細胞。

a bio-degradable material「生分解性の材料」微生物や酵素によって分解される材料。

the printed cells structure「プリントされた細胞組織」

34 **are looking into ways**「方法を研究し続けている」

the printing process「プリント製法」

35 **blood vessels**「血管」

cartilage「軟骨」

36 **whole organs**「完全な臓器」

Exercise 15-1: COMPREHENSION QUESTIONS

1. How does a 3D printer work?
   - (A) The object to be printed is copied in a mold, which is inserted into the printer.
   - (B) It builds an object layer by layer according to programmed instructions.
   - (C) The printer divides or slices the original object into horizontal layers.
   - (D) The process is accomplished by sensors and camera.

2. What kind of objects can be 3-D printed?
   - (A) Only objects made of hard materials such as metals
   - (B) In theory, any three-dimensional object
   - (C) Only objects that occur in nature
   - (D) Only objects that have been broken down into component parts

3. What is the first step in the 3-D printing process?
   - (A) Choosing the appropriate material
   - (B) Photographing the cross-cut tissue
   - (C) Applying the material layer by layer
   - (D) Slicing the original object into thousands of layers

4. What is one important benefit of 3-D printed prostheses?
   - (A) Greater similarity to human limbs
   - (B) Longer usefulness
   - (C) Reduced costs
   - (D) Greater mobility

5. What is the future likely to bring for 3-D printing?
   - (A) Greater advances in creating living tissue will be made.
   - (B) Artists will be put out of work.
   - (C) Costs for the printing machines and software will increase.
   - (D) 3D printers will eventually replace all conventional home-use printers.

Grammar Review

Relative
（関係詞）

関係代名詞　先行詞（名詞、代名詞）を修飾する形容詞節を導く。目的格は省略可。

格 先行詞	主格	所有格	目的格
人	who	whose	whom/who
事物	which	whose	which
人、事物	that		that

1. 先行詞が人の場合

Alexander Graham Bell is the scientist **who** invented the telephone.

(Alexander Graham Bell is a scientist. + He invented the telephone.)

I have a friend **whose** father is a police officer.

(I have a friend. + His/Her father is a police officer.)

Celebrities (**whom**/**who**) teens admire have to be careful about their behavior.

(Celebrities have to be careful about their behavior. + Teens admire them.)

2. 先行詞が事物の場合

The term "3D printer" refers to a device **that** forms objects based on three-dimentional (3-D) digital data.

Yutaka drives a car **whose** body has several dents.

I came up with an idea (**that**/**which**) everyone will like.

3. that が好まれる場合

① 先行詞に、最上級の形容詞、the first, the only, all, every, no などが付く時。

This is **the best** anime film **that** has been released this year.

② 先行詞が疑問代名詞の時。

Who that knows Carrie will believe she stole the money?

4. that が使われない場合

① 前置詞＋関係代名詞　This is the pen **with which** he wrote many great books.

② 継続用法　My mother, **who**'s into yoga, signed up for a new gym.

5. 関係代名詞としての what　先行詞を含み、「～もの / こと」を意味する。

I'll take back **what** I said yesterday.

関係副詞　先行詞（名詞、代名詞）を修飾する副詞節を導く。先行詞が省略可のこともある。

1. 先行詞が場所の場合

The hotel **where** we stayed in Sweden was made totally of ice.

2. 先行詞が時の場合

It was a time **when** smartphones were rare.

3. 先行詞が理由の場合

The reason **why** she did was unknown.

Exercise 15-2: Grammar Exercise

次の各文の空欄に最もふさわしい語を選びなさい。

1. I don't like to put off till tomorrow (　　　　) I can do today.
   (A) whose　　(B) what　　(C) which　　(D) why

2. He says he is going abroad soon, (　　　　) is a lie.
   (A) what　　(B) where　　(C) which　　(D) who

3. Paul was the only person (　　　　) I was acquainted with at the party.
   (A) that　　(B) what　　(C) which　　(D) whose

4. What is the name of that man (　　　　) son is a major league baseball player?
   (A) which　　(B) who　　(C) whose　　(D) whom

5. There are those (　　　　) believe in UFOs.
   (A) that　　(B) what　　(C) which　　(D) who

6. Which of these DVDs is the one (　　　　) you recommended to me?
   (A) that　　(B) what　　(C) whose　　(D) whom

7. The girl (　　　　) you spoke to is a famous novelist's daughter.
   (A) which　　(B) what　　(C) whose　　(D) whom

Exercise 15-3: Listening Practice

CD を聞いて空欄に正しい語を入れなさい。

The process has two main components. The first step is to create digital computer data (1.　　　　　　　　), in essence, tells the printing machine exactly what to do. The item to be replicated has to be divided into thousands of horizontal layers. (2.　　　　　　　　) step, called "slicing," is done by a computer-program or (3.　　　　　　　　) installed in a 3D printer. The information is then downloaded to the printer through a USB port or wireless Internet connection. The second step is the actual printing of the (4.　　　　　　　　) by applying successive layers of whatever material the printer is loaded with. 3D printers can produce objects from a wide range of materials, including malleable plastics, metals, metal alloys, and (5.　　　　　　　　).

著作権法上、無断複写・複製は禁じられています。

JAPAN EVOLUTION
進化する日本

B-882

1　　刷　2019 年 4 月 1 日

編 著 者　ジョアン・ペロケティ　JoAnn Parochetti
　　　　　千葉　　剛　　Tsuyoshi Chiba
　　　　　鄭　　耀星　　Yau-Sin Cheng
　　　　　清水　雅夫　　Masao Shimizu
　　　　　林　　孝憲　　Takanori Hayashi
　　　　　福岡　賢昌　　Takamasa Fukuoka

発 行 者　南雲　一範　　Kazunori Nagumo
発 行 所　株式会社　南雲堂
　　　　　〒 162-0801　東京都新宿区山吹町 361
　　　　　NAN'UN-DO Co., Ltd.
　　　　　361 Yamabuki-cho, Shinjyuku-ku, Tokyo 162-0801, Japan
　　　　　振替口座・00160-0-46863
　　　　　☎ 03-3268-2311
　　　　　編集者　加藤　敦

挿　　画　三輪美奈子
製　　版　日本ハイコム株式会社
装　　丁　銀月堂
コード　　ISBN978-4-523-17882-8　　C0082

Printed in Japan

E-mail　　nanundo@post.email.ne.jp
URL　　　http://www.nanun-do.co.jp/